D0850575

CAUGHT SNACKIN'

CAUGHT SNACKIN'

100 RECIPES
SIMPLE. FAST. FLAVORFUL.

weldon**owen**

weldon**owen**

an imprint of Insight Editions
P.O. Box 3088
San Rafael, CA 94912
www.weldonowen.com

CEO Raoul Goff
VP Publisher Roger Shaw
Editorial Director Katie Killebrew
Editorial Assistant Kayla Belser-Vernon
VP Manufacturing Alix Nicholaeff
Production Manager Joshua Smith

Weldon Owen would also like to thank Karen Levy.

First published in Great Britain in 2023 by Hamlyn, a division of Octopus Publishing Group Ltd.

ISBN: 979-8-88674-041-7

Manufactured in China
10 9 8 7 6 5 4 3 2 1

Insight Editions, in association with Roots of Peace, will plant two trees for each tree used in the manufacturing of this book. Roots of Peace is an internationally renowned humanitarian organization dedicated to eradicating land mines worldwide and converting war-torn lands into productive farms and wildlife habitats. Roots of Peace will plant two million fruit and nut trees in Afghanistan and provide farmers there with the skills and support necessary for sustainable land use.

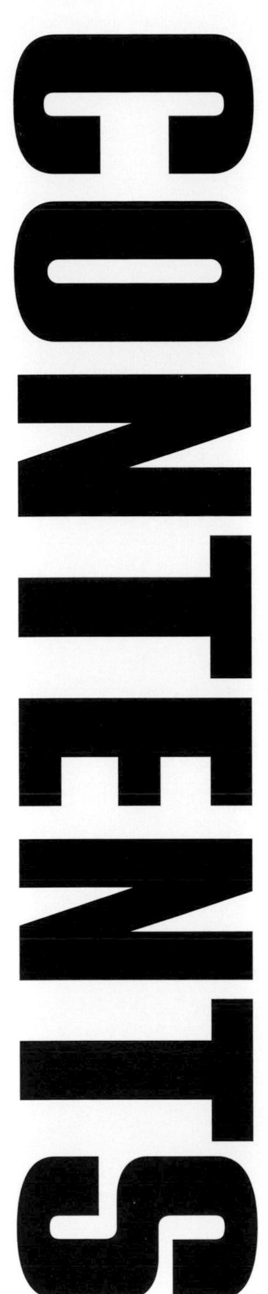
CONTENTS

INTRODUCTION

Caught Snackin' was launched on TikTok in April 2020 by the gang with a love for food! Two years later, we're the UK's fastest-growing TikTok channel, finessin' the game with recipe films that SLAP! You know like that?

OBVIOUSLY we had to roll through with Snackin' the cookbook. Snackin's where we started, but our cookbook covers all bases: from bougie brunches to simple lunches, Friday-night fakeouts to desserts that will make you TikTok famous.

Whether you're new to the kitchen or looking to level up, Caught will bless you! You don't need crazy chefileeni equipment or Gordon Ramsay tekz, just this book and good vibes.

This book is made for everyone: we believe that home-cooked food is the best way to eat, and anyone can do it with the right recipe. Our dishes are created first for deliciousness and second for ease; whether you're going all-in cooking for a crowd or lounging on the sofa with a bowl full of comfort food, we're bringing big flavors with zero stress. Our inspo came from all kinds of places and faces: TikTok, friends of Caught, food our families cooked, and random kitchen experiments gone RIGHT. It took us 730 DAYS and 1,500 dishes to get to where we are (with a few burned fingers and dud dishes along the way, not gonna lie). We're buzzing for you all to get cooking and eat this sensational food with us, you get me?

Just a few things for the gang to know...

The book is split into seven tasty chapters: Snackin' for the quick munch, Brunchin' for them strong starts to the day, Lunchin' for an upgrade from your meal deal, Dinin' for the winner dinners, Fakin' for the HACKS, Bakin' for them sweeeet treats and Sippin' for drinks too good not to share.

Our servings range from one to four people, but every appetite is different, so you do you. We don't judge! If you finesse a four-person recipe between two of you, it's cool. If you want to upsize or downsize, just adjust the servings to suit, or if you have an urge to freestyle and add your own spin on something, then we love to see it.

Importantly, our ingredients don't cost too much. Whether you're living the student life or making bank, our shopping lists suit everyone. Our food is inclusive and will put a smile on the face of everyone, from your grandma to the sweet one you want to impress. ESPECIALLY the SWEET ONE.

Right, we're talkin' too much. Time to roll up your sleeves and gear up for some serious snackin'. We hope you love this cookbook as much as we've loved making it; if you do, share the love with your friends and fam. Everyone's welcome in the Caught gang.

Whatever you're feeling, we got you! We hope the pages of this cookbook will soon be folded and flour-dusted from recipes you've gone back to again and again.

LET'S GOOOOO!

CAUGHT STREET GLOSSARY

YES PEOPLE, first things first. Anyone in the Snackin' gang will know how to speak our language, and if you're reading this book, you need to be educated with the lingo:

BANAYNAY
it's a banana, don't ask questions.

BANGING
amazing.

BASIC-B
generic.

BEV/BEVI
alcoholic/non-alcoholic drink.

BLESS or BLESSED
when something good happens.

BOUGIE
someone who be living that high life. Champagne, oysters and that.

CHEFILEENI
the correct way to say chef.

CHEEEEEEEEEEEEEESE
it just means cheese.

CHEF IT UP
cutting/slicing/cooking in general.

COTCHING
chilling.

G
mate, bro, hun, your nearest and dearest.

GLOW-UP
makeover.

MANDEM
the whole gang.

MAZZA
a madness.

MEADY
low-level/substandard.

PATTERNED
sort out/fix up.

PREE
look at.

RAGRETS
regrets, doh.

SAFE
cool/thanks.

SHOOK
this is like scared or shocked.

SHUBZ
party, gathering… anything with all the Caught gang!

SITCH
situation.

SLAPS
impressive, VERY good, delicious…

SWEET ONE
your lurver.

TEKZ
techniques.

TURNT
excited.

YES PEOPLE
a classic Caught Snackin' greeting (if you know you know).

Now that's done, WELCOME to the gang!

GET YOUR SHOP ON

Listen, every chefileeni needs them ingredient staples! Let us pattern you real quick...

OILS

- olive oil
- sunflower or vegetable oil

SEASONINGS

- black pepper
- Italian mixed dried herbs
- ketchup
- mustard
- salt
- soy sauce
- sweet chili sauce

SPICES

- chili powder
- curry powder
- fresh basil
- fresh cilantro
- garam masala
- garlic powder
- ground cinnamon
- ground cumin
- ground turmeric
- onion powder
- red pepper flakes
- red pepper powder
- smoked paprika

PANTRY

- baked beans
- basmati rice
- bouillon cubes (vegetable and chicken)
- breadcrumbs (panko)
- canned tomatoes
- chocolate hazelnut spread, such as Nutella
- corn puffs
- dried pasta
- garlic
- honey
- instant noodles
- long-grain rice
- onions
- salted potato chips
- sliced white bread
- speculoos cookies, such as Lotus
- speculoos spread
- sriracha
- tomato purée/paste
- tortilla chips
- tortilla wraps
- yeast extract spread, such as Marmite

BAKING

- all-purpose flour
- caster (superfine) sugar
- condensed milk
- dark chocolate
- instant cake mix
- Jell-O
- marshmallows
- milk chocolate
- powdered sugar
- self-rising flour
- white chocolate

REFRIGERATOR & FREEZER

- butter (salted and unsalted)
- chocolate ice cream
- cream (light and heavy)
- eggs
- ice cubes
- mayonnaise
- vanilla ice cream
- whole milk
- yogurt

PREP DEM TOOLS

All our recipes use easy equipment that every kitchen should already have (if you don't have an ovenproof dish, then it's a bit of a sticky one still), but here's a list of tools you'll need to get cheffin':

COOKWARE

- baking/cake pan
- baking sheet
- big roasting pan
- couple of decent ovenproof, nonstick frying pans: one shallow, one deep with a proper fitted lid
- deep saucepan with a fitted lid
- large ovenproof dish with a fitted lid
- muffin pan
- ovenproof ramekins

ELECTRICS

- electric mixer
- food processor or high-powered blender
- freezer
- hand-held stick blender
- microwave
- thermometer (handy for deep-frying - if you don't have one, check out our tip on page 17)

TOOLS

- ice-cube tray
- ovenproof bowls (we recommend 2-cup [0.5-L] and 4-cup [1-L] Pyrex heatproof glass bowls)
- piping bag with nozzles
- plastic squeezy sauce bottle with nozzle lid/piping bottle
- rolling pin
- shot measure
- small hand whisk

RANDOMS

- cupcake liners
- foil
- paper towels
- parchment paper
- plastic wrap
- tea towels

OK, now you're REALLY ready, so LET'S GO GO GOOOOO!

CAUGHT SNACKIN'

BASIC COOKING TIPS FOR BEGINNERS

My kitchen rookies, I see you! But don't worry, start with these kitchen tips and you'll soon be flexing awesome chefileeni skills!

HOW TO CHOP AN ONION

1. Using a large, sharp knife, remove the pointed end of the onion. Do not remove the root end, as this holds the onion layers together, making it easier to chop. Slicing the root end off will also release acidic juices, which make you cry.
2. Slice the onion in half horizontally (from end to end) and peel away the tough outer skin.
3. Place an onion half flat-side down and, holding your knife parallel to the work surface, carefully slice through the onion horizontally, taking your knife almost to the root end but not cutting through it completely, so that the onion half remains held together.
4. Now, make a series of cuts through the onion half lengthways, every ¼ inch (6 mm) or so, starting from the root end to the pointed end, again, keeping the root end intact.
5. Finally, holding your knife flat against the pointed end of the onion, slice against the cuts you have just made, resulting in fine dice. Chop along the onion, until you get ½–¾ inch (1- 2 cm) away from the root. Discard the root.
6. Repeat with the other half.

HOW TO SWEAT AN ONION

1. Heat 1–2 tablespoons olive oil in a frying pan or saucepan over medium–low heat and add the finely chopped onion. Season with salt and give it a stir to ensure the onion is coated in oil. Cook for 5 minutes or so, until the onion starts to turn translucent.
2. Tear off a square sheet of parchment paper and scrunch it up into a tight ball. Un–scrunch it and run it under water to dampen, then place it over the onions. It will act as a lid, and the moisture will help the onions sweat and stop them from burning. Reduce the heat to its lowest and allow the onions to sweat for 15–20 minutes, checking them every 5 minutes. The onions are cooked when they are fully translucent with a sweet aroma.

HOW TO MAKE

A SIMPLE TOMATO SAUCE

PREP TIME: **5 MINUTES** COOK TIME: **40 MINUTES**
DIFFICULTY: **EASY** SERVES: **2**
VEGAN

INGREDIENTS

1–2 tablespoons olive oil
½ onion, finely chopped
1 carrot, finely chopped
1 celery stalk, finely chopped
salt and pepper
2 garlic cloves, crushed
1 teaspoon Italian mixed dried herbs
1 tablespoon tomato purée/paste
1 (14–ounce [400–g]) can chopped tomatoes

METHOD

1. Heat the oil in a frying pan or saucepan over medium–low heat. Add the onion, carrot and celery and season with salt and pepper.
2. Sweat for 15 minutes, until the vegetables have softened, then add the garlic, dried herbs and tomato purée. Stir and cook for 5 minutes.
3. Pour over the chopped tomatoes and bring to a gentle simmer, stirring to combine. Cover and simmer the sauce for 20 minutes.
4. Season to taste and serve with pasta, use as a pizza base sauce, or allow to cool and save for another day. The sauce will keep in the refrigerator for 4 days, or in the freezer for up to 3 months.

You'll soon be flexing cool chefileeni skills!

A SIMPLE CHEESE SAUCE

PREP TIME: **5 MINUTES** COOK TIME: **5 MINUTES**
DIFFICULTY: **EASY** SERVES: **2**
VEGETARIAN

INGREDIENTS

2 tablespoons (28 g) unsalted butter
3 tablespoons (24 g) all-purpose flour
1–1¼ cups (240- 300 ml) milk
small pinch of ground nutmeg (optional)
1 cup (80 g) grated Cheddar cheese
salt and pepper

METHOD

1. Melt the butter in a saucepan over medium heat. Add the flour and whisk it into the butter until you have a thick, smooth paste. A sauce whisk (smaller than a normal whisk) is best for this. Cook the paste, whisking, for about 2 minutes until it turns a pale golden color. This is called a roux (pronounced roo) and is a classic base to all white sauces.
2. Slowly pour in the milk, a little at a time, whisking it into the roux before adding the next splash of milk. Once all the milk is incorporated, increase the heat a little and allow it to thicken slightly for 2 minutes before seasoning with salt and pepper.
3. If you wish to make a simple bechamel sauce, stop here, adding a small pinch of ground nutmeg. Great for homemade lasagna. If making a cheese sauce, simply add the grated Cheddar and stir over low heat until fully melted. For a simple macaroni and cheese, stir in par-boiled pasta shells and bake in the oven, topped with more cheese and breadcrumbs (see our hack on page 88 for how to make your own breadcrumbs).

Cheeeeeeeeeeeeeeesy

DEEP-FRYING

HOW TO CHECK THE TEMPERATURE OF OIL WITHOUT A THERMOMETER

When deep-frying, we recommend you use a temperature probe/cooking thermometer to check the oil temperature for safety and precision. These are easily purchased online or in kitchen shops and some of the larger supermarkets. However, if you don't have one, you can check the temperature using a less precise method... bread!

When the oil is hot (this will take 5–10 minutes over medium-low heat) drop in a cube of bread. The oil should bubble around the edges of the bread, and the bread will start to take on color as it cooks. The length of time the bread takes to turn a deep golden color is a good indicator of the temperature of the oil:

30 seconds = 325°F (160°C)
15 seconds = 350°F (180°C)
10 seconds = 375°F (190°C)

We recommend deep-frying with either vegetable oil or sunflower oil, as these have a high smoke point (so are less likely to burn).

SAFETY ADVICE

Don't own a deep-fryer? Use a large saucepan with a well-fitting lid. **Only use the lid when you have finished cooking and the saucepan has been removed from the heat.** Putting a lid on a pan of boiling oil can lead to dangerously high temperatures. Plus, it will result in sweaty, soggy food, and ruin that all-important crunch.

Keep a plate lined with paper towels nearby so that you can remove fried food and drain it without dripping hot oil all over the kitchen.

Use a metal slotted or wire-mesh spoon to remove food from hot oil.

NEVER mix water with hot oil, as this will cause a fire. Be sure to keep any water or other liquids away from the hot oil.

If the oil becomes too hot, the safest way to cool it down is to add cold oil and remove the pan from the heat.

Hot oil takes a long time to cool down (a few hours), so leave it in a safe place in your kitchen, covered with a well-fitting lid and out of reach of young children.

Always ensure there is an adult present when deep-frying. SAFE.

WILDFIRE HALLOUMI FRIES

PREP TIME: **10 MINUTES**
COOK TIME: **3 MINUTES**
DIFFICULTY: **MEDIUM**
SERVES: **2**
VEGETARIAN

Bless yourself with these crunchy, tangy, sensational halloumi fries... Look out for that chilli KICK.

INGREDIENTS

2 (9-ounce [250-g]) blocks halloumi cheese

1 (2-ounce [60-g]) bag hot chilli-flavored tortilla chips

½ cup (70 g) all-purpose flour

2 eggs, lightly beaten

2 cups (480 ml) vegetable oil, for deep-frying

METHOD

1. Pat dry the blocks of halloumi with paper towels and slice into chunky fries. You should get 6 fries from each block.
2. Using a rolling pin, the base of a heavy jar or a mortar, crush the tortilla chips to fine crumbs. Add to a shallow bowl.
3. Put the flour in a second shallow bowl and the eggs in a third.
4. Coat the halloumi fries in the flour, followed by the egg and finally the tortilla-chip crumbs. Lay the coated fries on a plate.
5. Heat the oil, in a deep saucepan with a well-fitting lid (see page 17), to 350°F (180°C) and fry the halloumi fries for 2½ minutes, until crisp and golden on the outside and melting in the middle. You may wish to do this in batches to avoid overcrowding the pan. Remove and drain on paper towels before serving.

PREP TIME: **10 MINUTES**
COOK TIME: **45 MINUTES**
DIFFICULTY: **EASY**
SERVES: **4**
VEGETARIAN

CHILE-CHEESE GARLIC BREAD

TRUST US! This chile-cheese garlic bread will elevate the vibes on the dinner table and spice up your night for sure.

INGREDIENTS

1 large garlic bulb

1 tablespoon olive oil

½ cup (110 g) salted butter, softened

2 tablespoons chopped parsley leaves

1 tablespoon red chile paste

1 large ciabatta loaf, about 10 ounces (280 g)

1 cup (100 g) grated mozzarella cheese

salt and pepper

METHOD

1. Preheat the oven to 400°F (200°C, or gas mark 6).
2. Slice the top off the bulb of garlic then drizzle the bulb with the olive oil and season with a pinch each of salt and pepper. Wrap in foil and bake for 30 minutes until soft in the middle. Leave the oven on.
3. In a bowl, combine the softened butter with the parsley, red chile paste and the roasted garlic cloves, squeezed from their skins. Mix with a fork until well combined.
4. Slice the ciabatta in half lengthways and score each half in a grid pattern. Spread generously with the spicy garlic butter and top with the grated mozzarella.
5. Bake for 15 minutes until crisp and bubbling.

Elevate the vibes on the dinner table

PREP TIME: **20 MINUTES**
COOK TIME: **12 MINUTES**
DIFFICULTY: **EASY**
SERVES: **3**
VEGAN

ICE-CUBE PIZZA BITES

For our pizza fans, this ice-cube hack will change your life, trust me! Mini deep-pan pizzas oozing with flavor.

INGREDIENTS

1 (14-ounce [400-g]) package packet of pre-rolled pizza dough or vegan shortcrust pastry

½ cup (60 g) sun-dried tomatoes, chopped

½ cup (40 g) grated vegan cheese

12 teaspoons vegan tomato pizza sauce (or see page 15)

4 tablespoons (32 g) all-purpose flour, to dust

2 tablespoons olive oil

1 tablespoon Italian mixed dried herbs

METHOD

1. Preheat the oven to 400°F (200°C, or gas mark 6) and line a baking sheet with parchment paper.
2. Slice the sheet of pizza dough or pastry in half widthwise, so you have 2 smaller rectangular sheets. Place 1 sheet over an ice-cube tray and gently push down into the individual molds, without breaking the sheet.
3. Divide the sun-dried tomatoes among the molds, then the vegan cheese, then add 1 teaspoon of pizza sauce to each mold (ice-cube trays generally have 12 molds).
4. Brush water over the dough or pastry at the edges of the cubes and lay the second sheet over the top, pressing it down to seal the edges.
5. Dust a workspace with the flour and turn over the ice-cube tray to turn out the contents. Use a knife or pizza cutter to slice into individual bites.
6. Arrange the bites on the prepared baking sheet, brush with the olive oil and top with the dried herbs. Bake for 12 minutes and serve.

SIZZLIN' OVEN–BAKED PIZZA DIP

PREP TIME: **5 MINUTES**
COOK TIME: **15 MINUTES**
DIFFICULTY: **EASY**
SERVES: **2**
VEGETARIAN

This recipe is IT: bubbling burrata with tangy pizza sauce IN DIP FORM. Flavors on flavors. Don't say we don't spoil you. No more basic hummus for you after you try this, G.

INGREDIENTS

- 1 cup (240 ml) tomato pizza sauce (or see page 15)
- 1 (5½–ounce [150 g]) ball Italian burrata, or mozzarella
- 1 garlic clove, crushed
- 1 tablespoon olive oil
- ¼ teaspoon red pepper flakes
- salt and pepper
- small handful of basil leaves
- 2–4 slices baked garlic bread, ideally Chile–Cheese Garlic Bread (see page 20), to serve

METHOD

1. Preheat the oven to 400°F (200°C, or gas mark 6).
2. Pour the tomato sauce into a small ovenproof dish and place the burrata in the center.
3. In a small bowl, combine the crushed garlic with the olive oil, red pepper flakes and salt and pepper, then drizzle over the dish.
4. Bake for 15 minutes until golden, molten and bubbling.
5. Sprinkle with basil and serve with the garlic bread for dipping.

you
Enjoy
Enjoy

SALT & PEPPER SQUID

PREP TIME: **10 MINUTES**
COOK TIME: **5 MINUTES**
DIFFICULTY: **EASY**
SERVES: **2**
FISH

This salt and pepps squid is so cute and crispy it's DANGEROUS. Best know we're gonna eat 40 without realizing...

INGREDIENTS

8 ounces (225 g) frozen raw squid tubes, or squid rings

6 tablespoons (48 g) cornstarch

200 ml (7 fl oz) vegetable oil

1 teaspoon chili powder

¼ teaspoon sea salt

¼ teaspoon ground black pepper

lime wedges, to serve

sweet chili sauce, for dipping

METHOD

1. Defrost the squid according to the package instructions.
2. Slice the squid tubes, if using, into rings, roughly ¾ inch (2 cm) wide. Pat the squid dry with paper towels.
3. Put the cornstarch into a shallow bowl. Toss the squid in the cornstarch.

Heat the oil in a frying pan over a medium-high heat and shallow-fry the squid for 2 minutes, turning halfway, until curled up, crisp and pale golden. (You may have to cook them in 2 batches, depending on the size of the pan.) Remove the squid pieces and drain on paper towels.

4. Combine the chili powder, salt and pepper in a medium-sized bowl and toss through the fried squid pieces, ensuring they are evenly coated in the seasoning.
5. Serve with lime wedges to squeeze and your favorite sweet chili dipping sauce.

TIP: You can find frozen squid tubes, or squid rings, in the frozen section of larger supermarkets.

PREP TIME: **5 MINUTES**
COOK TIME: **15 MINUTES**
DIFFICULTY: **EASY**
SERVES: **1**
VEGETARIAN

CHEESY POPCORN

The controversy over this dish is crazy, but don't hate us. TRY IT FIRST! Movie-night vibes all over this snack.

INGREDIENTS

2 tablespoons (28 g) unsalted butter

1 teaspoon yeast extract spread, such as Marmite

⅓ cup (30 g) finely grated Cheddar cheese

2 tablespoons vegetable oil

5 tablespoons (75 g) popcorn kernels

METHOD

1. Preheat the oven to 325ºF (160ºC, or gas mark 3). Line a baking sheet with parchment paper.
2. Melt the butter in a small saucepan over low heat. Stir in the yeast extract and grated Cheddar until well combined and smooth. Remove from the heat and set aside.
3. Heat the oil in a large, deep saucepan with a well-fitting lid set over medium-high heat. Add the popcorn kernels. Cover with the lid and give the pan a shake to ensure that the kernels are coated in the oil.
4. Shake the pan every minute or so. After a couple of minutes, the kernels will start to pop. Do not remove the lid.
5. Once the kernels are popping at a rapid pace, remove the pan from the heat and continue to shake every minute, but do not remove the lid until the popping has stopped.
6. When it is safe to remove the lid, stir in the cheesy butter, ensuring the popcorn is evenly coated.
7. Pour the cheesy popcorn onto the prepared baking sheet, and bake for 5 minutes until perfectly crisp and enjoy.

GARLIC & PARMESAN POTATO WEDGES

PREP TIME: **10 MINUTES**
COOK TIME: **1 HOUR**
DIFFICULTY: **EASY**
SERVES: **2**
VEGETARIAN

Don't be shocked by the whole garlic bulb, as roasting makes it sweet and caramelized: these cheesy herby garlicky wedges are BANGING!

INGREDIENTS

1 large garlic bulb
4 tablespoons olive oil
3 large baking potatoes, sliced into thick wedges
2 teaspoons fresh thyme leaves
3 tablespoons finely grated vegetarian Parmesan cheese
salt and pepper
your favorite dips, to serve

METHOD

1. Preheat the oven to 400°F (200°C, or gas mark 6).
2. Slice the top off the bulb of garlic, then drizzle the bulb with 1 tablespoon of the oil and season with a pinch each of salt and pepper. Wrap the bulb in kitchen foil and bake for 30 minutes until soft in the center.
3. Meanwhile, arrange the potato wedges on a large baking sheet.
4. Once cooked, squeeze the soft garlic cloves into a small bowl, discarding the skins. Combine with the remaining olive oil, half of the thyme leaves and 2 tablespoons of the grated Parmesan.
5. Drizzle the cheesy garlic oil over the potato wedges and massage it in with your hands, ensuring the wedges are well coated.
6. Bake for 30 minutes, turning halfway, until crisp and golden. Sprinkle with the remaining thyme leaves and Parmesan and serve with your favorite dips.

PREP TIME: **15 MINUTES**
COOK TIME: **15 MINUTES**
DIFFICULTY: **MEDIUM**
SERVES: **4**
VEGAN

SHROOM WINGS

These golden, crispy, meaty mushroom wings will leave you discombobulated when you realize they're VEGAN.

INGREDIENTS

- 1¼ cups (150 g) all-purpose flour
- 2 teaspoons smoked paprika
- 2 teaspoons Italian mixed dried herbs
- 1 teaspoon salt
- 2 teaspoons onion powder
- 2 teaspoons garlic powder
- 1 cup (240 ml) plant-based milk
- 1½ cups (180 g) breadcrumbs
- 10 ounces (280 g) baby portobello mushrooms, stalks removed, halved
- 1 quart (960 ml) vegetable oil, for deep-frying
- vegan barbecue-style sauce, for dipping

METHOD

1. In a large mixing bowl, combine the flour, smoked paprika, dried herbs, salt, onion powder, garlic powder and plant-based milk. Whisk this batter until it is thick and smooth.
2. Put the breadcrumbs into a medium-sized bowl.
3. Coat the mushroom halves in the batter, followed by the breadcrumbs, and place on a plate or wire rack.
4. Heat the oil, in a deep saucepan with a well-fitting lid, to 350°F (180°C) over medium-low heat. (See page 17 for deep-frying hacks.)
5. Fry the mushrooms in batches for 3 minutes, or until golden and crisp. Remove from the oil and drain on paper towel. Serve with your favorite vegan barbecue-style sauce.

TIP:
Want to make your own breadcrumbs? See our hack on page 88.

SHRIMP TOAST ROLL-UPS

PREP TIME: **20 MINUTES**
COOK TIME: **12 MINUTES**
DIFFICULTY: **EASY**
SERVES: **4**
FISH

Crispy, crunchy and all-round VIBES! I'm tucking these juicy shrimp into their toasty bread-bed and they're getting munched immediately.

INGREDIENTS

6 ounces (170 g) jumbo shrimp
1 teaspoon salt
1 teaspoon ground white pepper
1 teaspoon ground ginger
1 teaspoon soy sauce
3 eggs, 1 separated
12 white bread slices
4 tablespoons white sesame seeds
2 tablespoons black sesame seeds
3 tablespoons unsalted butter
sweet chili sauce, for dipping

METHOD

1. Put the shrimp, salt, white pepper, ginger, soy sauce and egg white in a food processor or high-powered blender and blend to a smooth paste. Cover and place in the refrigerator until needed.
2. Stack the slices of bread on a board and slice off the crusts. Make breadcrumbs with the crusts, for use at a later date (see page 88).
3. Use a rolling pin to flatten a slice of bread, then evenly spread it with 1½ teaspoons of the shrimp paste. Combine the white and black sesame seeds in a small bowl, sprinkle a small pinch over the top of the bread slice, then roll it up tightly into a cigar. Repeat to flatten, fill and roll all the bread slices.
4. Whisk the remaining eggs and egg yolk in a shallow bowl. Dip the roll-ups in the egg, turning to coat, then scatter over the remaining sesame seeds.
5. Melt the butter in a frying pan over medium-low heat and fry the shrimp toast roll-ups for 10–12 minutes, turning regularly, until evenly golden. Serve with sweet chili dipping sauce.

PREP TIME: **10 MINUTES**
COOK TIME: **35 MINUTES**
DIFFICULTY: **EASY**
SERVES: **4**
MEAT

CANDIED TWIST BACON

Have you ever heard the phrase "Don't get your bacon in a twist"? No, us neither, but these crispy candied bacon twists SLAP!

INGREDIENTS

8 ounces (224 g) bacon strips
1 teaspoon light brown sugar
½ teaspoon cayenne pepper

METHOD

1. Preheat the oven to 400°F (200°C, or gas mark 6). Line a baking sheet with foil.
2. Twist the bacon slices into tight ringlets and arrange them on the prepared baking sheet.
3. Combine the light brown sugar and cayenne pepper in a small bowl and sprinkle this over the bacon twists.
4. Bake for 35 minutes, until golden and crisp. (It takes this long for them to cook as they are tightly twisted.)
5. Remove the twists from the oven and place on some paper towels to drain off any excess fat. Serve with ketchup or brown sauce, add to your next Full English (see page 71) or go double-bacon *and* dip into a soft-boiled egg yolk with our Bacon Egg Cups (see page 76).

TIP:
To elevate your twists, wrap the bacon around cheese strings and enjoy these stretchy treats!

RED-HOT POPCORN CHICKEN

PREP TIME: **15 MINUTES**
COOK TIME: **15 MINUTES**
DIFFICULTY: **MEDIUM**
SERVES: **2**
MEAT

Crispy, spicy and fierce finger food for all the gang at the shubz.

INGREDIENTS

1 (2-ounce [60-g]) bag hot chili-flavored corn puffs

6 tablespoons (48 g) all-purpose flour

½ teaspoon cayenne pepper

½ teaspoon smoked paprika

¼ teaspoon garlic powder

¼ teaspoon salt

1 egg

2 chicken breasts, chopped into 1-inch (2.5-cm) cubes

2 cups (480 ml) vegetable oil, for deep-frying (optional)

Buffalo sauce, for dipping

METHOD

1. If baking the chicken, preheat the oven to 350°F (180°C, or gas mark 4).
2. Using a rolling pin, the base of a heavy jar or a mortar, gently crush the corn puffs into fine crumbs. Pour the crumbs into a bowl.
3. In another bowl, combine the flour, cayenne pepper, smoked paprika, garlic powder and salt. Lightly beat the egg in a third bowl.
4. Toss the chicken in the seasoned flour, ensuring it is well coated. Next, turn the pieces in the egg, followed by the corn-puff crumbs.
5. If deep-frying, heat the oil, in a deep saucepan with a well-fitting lid, to 350°F (180°C) over medium-low heat. Once the oil reaches this temperature, reduce the heat to low. Fry the chicken in batches for 3½ minutes until evenly golden. Remove from the oil and drain on paper towels. Let the chicken cool for at least 5 minutes before digging in. (See page 17 for deep-frying hacks.)
6. Alternatively, bake the popcorn chicken in the preheated oven, on a wire rack set over an oven tray, for 15 minutes.
7. Serve with Buffalo sauce, for dipping.

TORTILLA CHIPS 3 WAYS

Whether you're feeling sweet, savory or spicy, we got you. What's our favorite of the three? Pass.

CINNAMON SUGAR

PREP TIME: **5 MINUTES**

COOK TIME: **5 MINUTES**

DIFFICULTY: **EASY**

SERVES: **2**

VEGETARIAN

INGREDIENTS

1 teaspoon sugar

½ teaspoon ground cinnamon

3 small flour tortillas

2 tablespoons (28 g) salted butter, melted

3 tablespoons chocolate and hazelnut spread, such as Nutella, melted

METHOD

1. Preheat the oven to 325ºF (160ºC, or gas mark 3). Line a baking sheet with parchment paper.
2. Combine the sugar and cinnamon in a small bowl.
3. Pile up the tortillas on a board and slice into 8 even wedges, making 24 chips.
4. Lay out the tortilla chips on the prepared baking sheet and brush with the melted butter.
5. Sprinkle with the cinnamon sugar and bake for 5–6 minutes until golden and crisp.
6. Serve with the melted chocolate and hazelnut spread, for dipping.

SMOKIN'

PREP TIME: **5 MINUTES**

COOK TIME: **5 MINUTES**

DIFFICULTY: **EASY**

SERVES: **4**

VEGAN

INGREDIENTS

1 teaspoon smoked paprika

½ teaspoon cayenne pepper

¼ teaspoon salt

3 small flour tortillas

1 tablespoon olive oil

salsa, to serve (optional)

METHOD

1. Preheat the oven to 325ºF (160ºC, or gas mark 3). Line a baking sheet with parchment paper.
2. Combine the smoked paprika, cayenne pepper and salt in a small bowl.
3. Pile up the tortillas on a board and slice into 8 even wedges, making 24 chips.
4. Lay out the tortilla chips on the prepared baking sheet and brush with the olive oil.
5. Sprinkle with the spice mix and bake for 5–6 minutes until golden and crisp.
6. Serve with salsa, for dipping, if you like.

GARLIC CHEESE

PREP TIME: **10 MINUTES**

COOK TIME: **5 MINUTES**

DIFFICULTY: **EASY**

SERVES: **4**

VEGETARIAN

INGREDIENTS

1 teaspoon garlic powder

2 teaspoons Italian mixed dried herbs

2 tablespoons finely grated vegetarian Parmesan cheese, or Grana Padano cheese

3 small flour tortillas

2 tablespoons olive oil

pinch of salt

guacamole, to serve (optional)

METHOD

1. Preheat the oven to 325ºF (160ºC, or gas mark 3). Line a baking sheet with parchment paper.
2. Combine the garlic powder, Italian herbs, cheese and a pinch of salt in a small bowl.
3. Pile up the tortillas on a board and slice the pile into 8 even wedges, making 24 chips.
4. Lay out the tortilla chips on the prepared baking sheet and brush with the olive oil.
5. Sprinkle with the garlic and cheese mixture and bake in the oven for 5–6 minutes until golden and crisp.
6. Serve with guacamole, for dipping, if you like.

GARLIC CHEESE
CINNAMON SUGAR

SMOKIN'

PREP TIME: **5 MINUTES**
COOK TIME: **10 MINUTES**
DIFFICULTY: **EASY**
SERVES: **4**
VEGETARIAN

CANDY STORE CHOCOLATE BARK

We're taking indulgence to a whole new level with a mash-up of nostalgic sweeties. Keep chewing for them explosions of popping candy!

INGREDIENTS

8 ounces (224 g) white chocolate chips
8 ounces (224 g) milk chocolate chips
handful of salted pretzels
handful of jelly beans
1 (¼-ounce [7-g]) package popping candy
1 (1.7-ounce [47-g]) bag M&M's
1 small favorite milk chocolate bar, broken into pieces

METHOD

1. Melt the white chocolate and milk chocolate separately in heatproof bowls, each set over a saucepan of gently simmering water.
2. Line a large baking sheet with parchment paper and pour over the melted milk chocolate. Using a spatula, spread the chocolate out into a rectangle, about 12 x 8 inches (30 x 20 cm).
3. Spoon over the melted white chocolate, ensuring you leave space between each spoonful so you can see the contrast between the milk and white chocolate. Swirl a toothpick or skewer through the chocolate to create a marbling effect.
4. Scatter over the remaining ingredients for a colorful and textured chocolate bark, then transfer to the refrigerator for 30 minutes to set.
5. Roughly chop into bite-sized pieces to serve.

CHURROS BITES

PREP TIME: **10 MINUTES**
COOK TIME: **15–20 MINUTES**
DIFFICULTY: **MEDIUM**
SERVES: **4**
VEGETARIAN

These fluffy and sugary churros finessed with a melted chocolate dip will make your heart sing, G – trust me.

INGREDIENTS

1 cup (240 ml) water
4 tablespoons (56 g) unsalted butter, cubed
¼ cup (50 g) caster sugar
¼ teaspoon salt
2 cups (240 g) all-purpose flour
¼ teaspoon baking soda
4 cups (960 ml) vegetable oil, for deep-frying
½ teaspoon ground cinnamon
melted chocolate, to serve (optional)

METHOD

1. In a saucepan, combine the water, butter, 2 teaspoons of the caster sugar and the salt. Place over low heat to allow the butter to melt, then take off the heat.
2. Sift the flour and baking soda into a large mixing bowl and make a well in the center. Pour in the melted butter mixture and beat, quickly, with a wooden spoon, until you have a smooth, thick dough.
3. Spoon the dough into a piping bag fitted with a large star-shaped piping nozzle and set aside.
4. Heat the oil, in a deep saucepan with a well-fitting lid, to 350°F (180°C) over medium-low heat. Line a plate with paper towels and place this near the saucepan. (See page 17 for deep-frying hacks.)
5. Carefully pipe the dough into the oil, using kitchen scissors to cut it into 1-2 inch (2.5-5 cm) churros as you pipe. Fry the churros in batches for 5-6 minutes until golden and crisp. Remove from the oil with a slotted spoon and drain on the prepared plate.
6. Mix the remaining caster sugar with the ground cinnamon in a shallow bowl and roll the churros in it, ensuring they are well coated. Serve with a small bowl of melted chocolate for dipping, if you like.

PREP TIME: **5 MINUTES**
COOK TIME: **15 MINUTES**
DIFFICULTY: **MEDIUM**
SERVES: **4**
VEGAN

DIY HONEYCOMB

You know them ones where you're craving a sweet treat but don't wanna leave the house? This is a four-ingredient pantry winner for lazy nights in.

INGREDIENTS

1 cup (200 g) caster sugar
5 tablespoons (75 g) light corn syrup
1 tablespoon water
1 tablespoon baking soda

METHOD

1. Line an 8-inch (20-cm) square baking pan with parchment paper.
2. Put the caster sugar, corn syrup and water into a large saucepan and gently melt over low heat. This should take about 10 minutes.
3. When the sugar has completely melted, increase the temperature to medium-low heat and gently simmer for 5 minutes, or until the mixture turns a pale amber color.
4. Remove from the heat and sift in the baking soda, then stir the mixture vigorously with a wooden spoon until the baking soda is fully incorporated. It will foam up and expand quite rapidly.
5. Transfer the mixture to the prepared baking pan and set aside for about 30 minutes to cool and harden.
6. Once the honeycomb is set, turn it out of the pan, peel away the parchment paper, then break into bite-sized pieces. Delicious on its own, dipped into melted chocolate and left to set, or crumbled over ice cream.

CAUGHT BRUNCHIN'

CAUGHT'S TOP EGG–COOKING HACKS

These eggcellent hacks are no yolk. Absolute cracking tips 'n' tricks from yours truly. Don't say we don't spoil you lot.

EGG SEPARATION HACK

PREP TIME: **1 MINUTE**
COOK TIME: **NONE**
DIFFICULTY: **EASY**
SERVES: **1**
VEGETARIAN

INGREDIENTS

1 egg

METHOD

1. Crack the egg into a small bowl.
2. Remove the lid from a clean, empty plastic bottle and gently squeeze the sides of the bottle. Hold the opening over the egg yolk and release your pressure on the bottle. The yolk will get sucked into the bottle opening, separating it from the white.
3. Squeeze the bottle to release the yolk into a separate bowl or container.

EGG POCKET HACK

PREP TIME: **1 MINUTE**

COOK TIME: **5 MINUTES**

DIFFICULTY: **EASY**

SERVES: **1**

VEGETARIAN

INGREDIENTS

½ tablespoon vegetable oil

1 egg

METHOD

1. Heat the oil in a frying pan over medium heat.
2. Separate the egg white from the yolk (using the Egg Separation Hack shown opposite) and add the white to the pan. Swirl the pan to ensure that the egg white is evenly distributed.
3. Once the egg white is cooked through, gently add the yolk into the center of the egg white and fold over the sides, sealing the yolk into a neat pocket. Cook for 1 minute, then flip and cook for a further minute.
4. Serve on buttered toast, cutting into the pocket for that runny yolk deliciousness!

LADLE POACHED EGGS

PREP TIME: **NONE**

COOK TIME: **6 MINUTES**

DIFFICULTY: **EASY**

SERVES: **1**

VEGETARIAN

INGREDIENTS

½ teaspoon vegetable oil

1 egg

METHOD

1. Bring a small saucepan of water to a boil.
2. Lightly oil a stainless-steel ladle with the oil and crack the egg into it. Lower the ladle into the boiling water so that the water comes up the sides but doesn't overflow on to the egg.
3. Hold the ladle in the simmering water for 4–6 minutes, or until cooked through.
4. Serve on toast with avocado, red pepper flakes and salt and pepper, if you like.

MICROWAVE "POACHED" EGGS

PREP TIME: **1 MINUTES**

COOK TIME: **1½ MINUTES**

DIFFICULTY: **EASY**

SERVES: **1**

VEGETARIAN

INGREDIENTS

1 teaspoon white wine vinegar

1 egg

METHOD

1. Fill a mug with boiling water and add the vinegar. Crack the egg into the mug and microwave on high for 1½ minutes.
2. Drain the egg and serve on buttered toast, with avocado, if you like.

MICROWAVE "BAKED" EGGS

PREP TIME: **1 MINUTE**

COOK TIME: **1½–2 MINUTES**

DIFFICULTY: **EASY**

SERVES: **1**

VEGETARIAN

INGREDIENTS

½ teaspoon vegetable oil

1 egg

salt and pepper

METHOD

1. Oil the inside of a mug with the vegetable oil and crack in the egg. Season with salt and pepper and microwave on high for 1½–2 minutes until the egg is cooked through.
2. Run a butter knife around the edge of the egg to release it from the mug and serve on toast.
3. You could also try putting mashed avocado, baked beans or grated cheese in the mug before cracking the egg over. Microwave on high for 1½–2 minutes and enjoy straight out of the mug.

STRIPED CHEESE OMELETTE

PREP TIME: **1 MINUTE** COOK TIME: **10 MINUTES**

DIFFICULTY: **EASY** SERVES: **1**

VEGETARIAN

INGREDIENTS

3 eggs

1 teaspoon unsalted butter

¼ cup (20 g) grated Cheddar cheese

salt and pepper

METHOD

1. Separate the eggs (see page 52) and melt the butter in a large frying pan over a medium heat.
2. Whisk the yolks and pour them into the pan, swirling them so they are evenly distributed across the base of the pan. Cook for about 1 minute, until set, then remove the pan from the heat.
3. Using a small, sharp knife, cut vertical lines in the yolk so that you have strips roughly ¾ inch (2cm) wide. Carefully peel away every other strip of egg yolk (eating it as you go).
4. Return the pan to the heat and pour over the egg whites. As the whites cook, they will fill the gaps in the yolk, leaving distinct stripes.
5. When the egg whites are almost set, sprinkle over the Cheddar and season with salt and pepper. Fold in each side of the omelette to cover the filling. Cook for about 30 seconds, then slide a spatula underneath and quickly flip. Cook for a further 30 seconds until the cheese is melty.
6. Serve immediately and enjoy this sensational breakfast!

These eggcellent hacks are no yolk

SHAKEN UP "SHAKSHUKA"

PREP TIME: **10 MINUTES**
COOK TIME: **25 MINUTES**
DIFFICULTY: **EASY**
SERVES: **4**
VEGETARIAN

As if one pesto isn't enough, we went in with the red AND green. Why? You know why. This shakshuka will shake up everyone at the shubz, trust us.

INGREDIENTS

1 tablespoon olive oil
1 onion, finely chopped
4 tablespoons vegetarian red pesto
2 (14-ounce [400-g]) cans chopped tomatoes
4 eggs
2 avocados, sliced
1 cup (100 g) crumbled feta or goat cheese
small pinch of red pepper flakes
2 tablespoons vegetarian green pesto
crusty garlic bread, to serve (optional, for homemade see page 20)

METHOD

1. Heat the olive oil in a large, deep frying pan with a well-fitting lid over medium heat.
2. Reduce the heat to medium-low and sweat the onion for 5 minutes, until starting to turn translucent.
3. Add the red pesto and chopped tomatoes and stir to combine. Bring to a simmer and cook for 10 minutes to thicken the sauce.
4. Use a spoon to create 4 wells in the sauce and crack in the eggs. Top the shakshuka with the sliced avocado, crumbled cheese and red pepper flakes, then cover and simmer for a further 10 minutes, or until the eggs are cooked through.
5. Add a few dollops of green pesto and serve with crusty garlic bread for dipping, if you like.

PREP TIME: **15 MINUTES**
COOK TIME: **20–25 MINUTES**
DIFFICULTY: **EASY**
SERVES: **4 (MAKES 8)**
FISH

SMOKED SALMON & POTATO MUFFINS

Don't get it twisted, muffins can be savory too, you know? Smoked salmon, 'cause we fancy, finessed with good flavors. Why not indulge in a muffin first thing in the AM?

INGREDIENTS

6 eggs, lightly beaten

2 tablespoons milk

1 large russet potato, peeled and chopped into ½-inch (1-cm) cubes

5 ounces (150 g) hot-smoked salmon, torn into chunks

2 teaspoons finely chopped chives, plus extra to serve

¼ teaspoon salt

¼ teaspoon cracked black pepper

3 teaspoons olive oil

METHOD

1. Preheat the oven to 350°F (180°C, or gas mark 4) and line a muffin pan with 8 paper liners.
2. Combine the eggs and milk in a large bowl, then add the potato, salmon, chives, salt and pepper.
3. Distribute the mixture evenly among the muffin liners. Bake for 20-25 minutes until golden and risen. Sprinkle with more chives and serve immediately. Alternatively, wait until cooled and then store in an airtight container in the refrigerator (to keep the fish fresh) for up to 2 days.

TIP: You can make these the day before, then eat them chilled or warmed through in the oven.

FIVE-MINUTE MICROWAVE EGGS ROYALE

PREP TIME: **5 MINUTES**
COOK TIME: **5 MINUTES**
DIFFICULTY: **EASY**
SERVES: **2**
FISH

Do you want to be classy? But only have 5 minutes before you need to leave? NO STRESS G, this tasty hollandaise egg hack will get you out the door with happy taste buds and sophistication.

INGREDIENTS

4 tablespoons (56 g) unsalted butter
6 eggs
¼ cup (60 ml) heavy cream
1 lemon, cut into 4 wedges
¼ teaspoon salt
pinch of black pepper
4 teaspoons white wine vinegar
4 English muffins, toasted and buttered
3½ ounces (100 g) smoked salmon or trout
cayenne pepper

METHOD

1. Place the butter into a medium bowl and microwave on high for 30 seconds until melted.
2. Separate 2 of the eggs, reserving the egg whites for another recipe.
3. In a small bowl, whisk together the 2 egg yolks with the cream, juice from one of the lemon wedges, and salt and pepper. Pour the egg mixture into the melted butter and whisk until well combined.
4. Return to the microwave for 1–2 minutes, stopping every 15 seconds to whisk the mixture. This hollandaise sauce is ready once it has thickened to a creamy, custard-like consistency. Cover and set aside.
5. Fill 4 mugs with boiling water and add 1 teaspoon of the vinegar to each. Crack an egg into each mug and microwave, 2 mugs at a time, on high for 1½ minutes.
6. Meanwhile, top the muffins with the salmon or trout. Drain the eggs and serve on the muffins, topped with the hollandaise, a pinch of cayenne pepper and the remaining lemon wedges on the side for squeezing over.

PREP TIME: **5 MINUTES**
COOK TIME: **20 MINUTES**
DIFFICULTY: **EASY**
SERVES: **2**
VEGETARIAN

COOKIE DOUGH BAKED OATS

No better start to your day than these BANGING cookie dough oats! The sugar kick be real.

INGREDIENTS

1 banana

1¼ cups (100 g) old-fashioned oats, pulsed into a powder in a food processor

2 tablespoons honey

1 tablespoon smooth peanut butter (optional)

½ teaspoon baking powder

¼ teaspoon salt

½ cup (120 ml) milk (dairy or plant-based)

¼ cup (45 g) chocolate chips

METHOD

1. Preheat the oven to 350°F (180°C, or gas mark 4).
2. Mash the banana with a fork in a medium bowl, then add the oatmeal, honey, peanut butter (if using), baking powder, salt, milk and half the chocolate chips. Stir to combine, then pour into 2 small ovenproof ramekins.
3. Top with the remaining chocolate chips and bake for 20 minutes until risen and golden. Serve immediately.

PILE-UP POTATO NACHOS

PREP TIME: **15 MINUTES**
COOK TIME: **30–40 MINUTES**
DIFFICULTY: **EASY**
SERVES: **4**
VEGAN

Hear us out: swap tortilla chips for crispy potato slices and load up with black beans, spicy jalapeños and, of course, PLENTY of cheese and avo. You won't be disappointed with this one.

INGREDIENTS

8 russet or sweet potatoes, finely sliced
3 tablespoons olive oil
2 teaspoons smoked paprika
¼ teaspoon salt
2½ cups (200 g) grated vegan cheese
1 (14-ounce [400-g]) can black beans, drained
2 avocados, sliced
2 jalapeños, sliced
⅓ cup (80 g) vegan yogurt (optional)

To serve (all optional)
cilantro
lime wedges

METHOD

1. Preheat the oven to 375ºF (190ºC, or gas mark 5). Line a baking sheet with parchment paper and set aside for later.
2. In a large bowl, toss the potato slices in the oil, smoked paprika and salt.
3. Lay the potato slices across 1–2 baking sheets and bake for 20–25 minutes, or until golden and starting to crisp up.
4. Once cooked, pile half the potato nachos on to the prepared baking sheet. Top with half the grated cheese, half the black beans, half the avocados and half the jalapeños.
5. Layer over the rest of the potato nachos and top with the remaining cheese, beans, avocados and jalapeños. Return to the oven for 10–15 minutes until everything is warmed through and the cheese is melted.
6. Serve on the tray, or transfer to a serving platter and top with dollops of yogurt. Scatter with cilantro and lime wedges, if you like.

CROQUE MADAME CROISSANT BAKE

PREP TIME: **10 MINUTES**
COOK TIME: **15 MINUTES**
DIFFICULTY: **EASY**
SERVES: **4**
MEAT

This dish tastes banging and is a sick way to turn it up when sharing with the mandem. Fill croissants with honey-roast ham and cheese, cover with creamy sauce, bake 'til bubblin' and whack a crispy fried egg on top... OOOOFT.

INGREDIENTS

4 croissants
4 thick slices honey-roast ham
1 cup (100 g) grated Cheddar cheese
6 eggs
4 teaspoons (20 ml) heavy cream
½ cup (120 ml) whole milk
¼ teaspoon salt
¼ teaspoon cracked black pepper
knob of salted butter

METHOD

1. Preheat the oven to 350°F (180°C, or gas mark 4).
2. Slice the croissants in half and fill with the slices of ham and half the cheese. Arrange the filled croissants on a rimmed baking sheet.
3. Lightly beat 2 of the eggs in a medium-sized bowl, then stir in the heavy cream, whole milk, remaining Cheddar and salt and pepper.
4. Pour the egg mixture over the croissants and bake for 12 minutes until the cheese is melted and bubbling.
5. Meanwhile, melt the butter in a large frying pan over a medium-high heat and fry the remaining 4 eggs.
6. Remove the croissant bake from the oven and serve immediately, with each portion topped with a crispy fried egg.

PREP TIME: **5 MINUTES + AT LEAST 1 HOUR MARINATING**
COOK TIME: **30 MINUTES**
DIFFICULTY: **EASY**
SERVES: **2**
MEAT

FROSTED-FLAKE CHICKEN WAFFLES

Just TASTE the marriage between sweet and savory, flavors made in holy matrimony. Don't ask questions, make this sensational frosted-flake chicken and waffles and thank us later.

INGREDIENTS

1¼ cups (300 ml) buttermilk
2 tablespoons hot sauce
1 teaspoon garlic powder
2 chicken breasts, each cut into 6 strips
10 ounces (280 g) frosted flakes
4 shop-bought Belgian waffles
salt
maple syrup, to serve

METHOD

1. Combine the buttermilk, hot sauce, garlic powder and a large pinch of salt in a medium-sized bowl.
2. Add the chicken to the seasoned buttermilk, ensuring the strips are well coated. Cover and allow to marinate in the refrigerator for 1 hour or, ideally, overnight.
3. Preheat the oven to 400°F (200°C, or gas mark 6).
4. Gather the frosted flakes inside a clean tea towel and use a rolling pin to gently roll and bash the flakes into fine crumbs.
5. Coat the marinated chicken strips in the frosted-flake crumbs and place on a wire rack set over a rimmed baking sheet. Bake for 30 minutes, or until golden brown, flipping halfway.
6. Heat the waffles according to the package instructions.
7. Stack the chicken on the waffles and serve, drizzled generously with maple syrup.

SHEET-PAN FULL ENGLISH

PREP TIME: **5 MINUTES**
COOK TIME: **40 MINUTES**
DIFFICULTY: **EASY**
SERVES: **4**
MEAT

Forget pots and pans: the Full English is a sheet-pan ting from now onwards. Get stuck in with the big boi with all the British breakfast staples! Do not think of skipping the buttered toast or the red or brown sauce on the side.

INGREDIENTS

4 bacon slices

4 pork sausages

8 store-bought hash browns

7 ounces (224 g) cremini chestnut mushrooms, quartered

10 cherry tomatoes

1 (8-ounce [224-g]) can baked beans

4 eggs

handful of parsley leaves, roughly chopped, optional

buttered toast, to serve

METHOD

1. Preheat the oven to 400°F (200°C, or gas mark 6).
2. Arrange the bacon, sausages, hash browns, mushrooms and cherry tomatoes on a large rimmed baking sheet. Add the baked beans in large spoonfuls, spaced out across the tray.
3. Transfer to the oven for 30 minutes or until the vegetables are tender and the sausages are golden brown and cooked through.
4. Remove the baking sheet from the oven and make 4 wells with a spoon. Crack the eggs into the wells and return to the oven for 10 minutes, or until the egg whites are firm.
5. Sprinkle with chopped parsley (if using) and serve with buttery toast and your favorite breakfast sauce.

PREP TIME: **5 MINUTES**
COOK TIME: **10 MINUTES**
DIFFICULTY: **EASY**
SERVES: **1**
VEGETARIAN

PANCAKE CEREAL

Mini fluffy pancakes, marshmallows and cookies floating in chocolate milk? Best believe it, 'cos we went there. A sugary sweet start to your day for them ones when muesli isn't an option.

INGREDIENTS

- 1 egg
- 1 cup (120 g) all-purpose flour
- ⅔ cup (160 ml) whole milk
- 1 teaspoon maple or light corn syrup
- 2 tablespoons mini marshmallows (optional)
- 1 tablespoon mini cookies (optional)
- chocolate milk, to serve

METHOD

1. In a bowl, beat the egg, flour, milk and syrup into a smooth batter and pour it into a squeezy sauce bottle fitted with a nozzle.
2. Heat a nonstick frying pan over medium heat.
3. Pipe some of the batter into the pan, in rounds about ¾ inch (2 cm) wide. Cook for 20 seconds on each side, flipping with a butter knife, until evenly golden. You will have to repeat this process 3–4 times to use up all the batter.
4. Allow the pancakes to cool on paper towels, then put them in a cereal bowl. Scatter with the mini marshmallows and mini cookies for added texture, if you like.
5. Serve with chocolate milk.

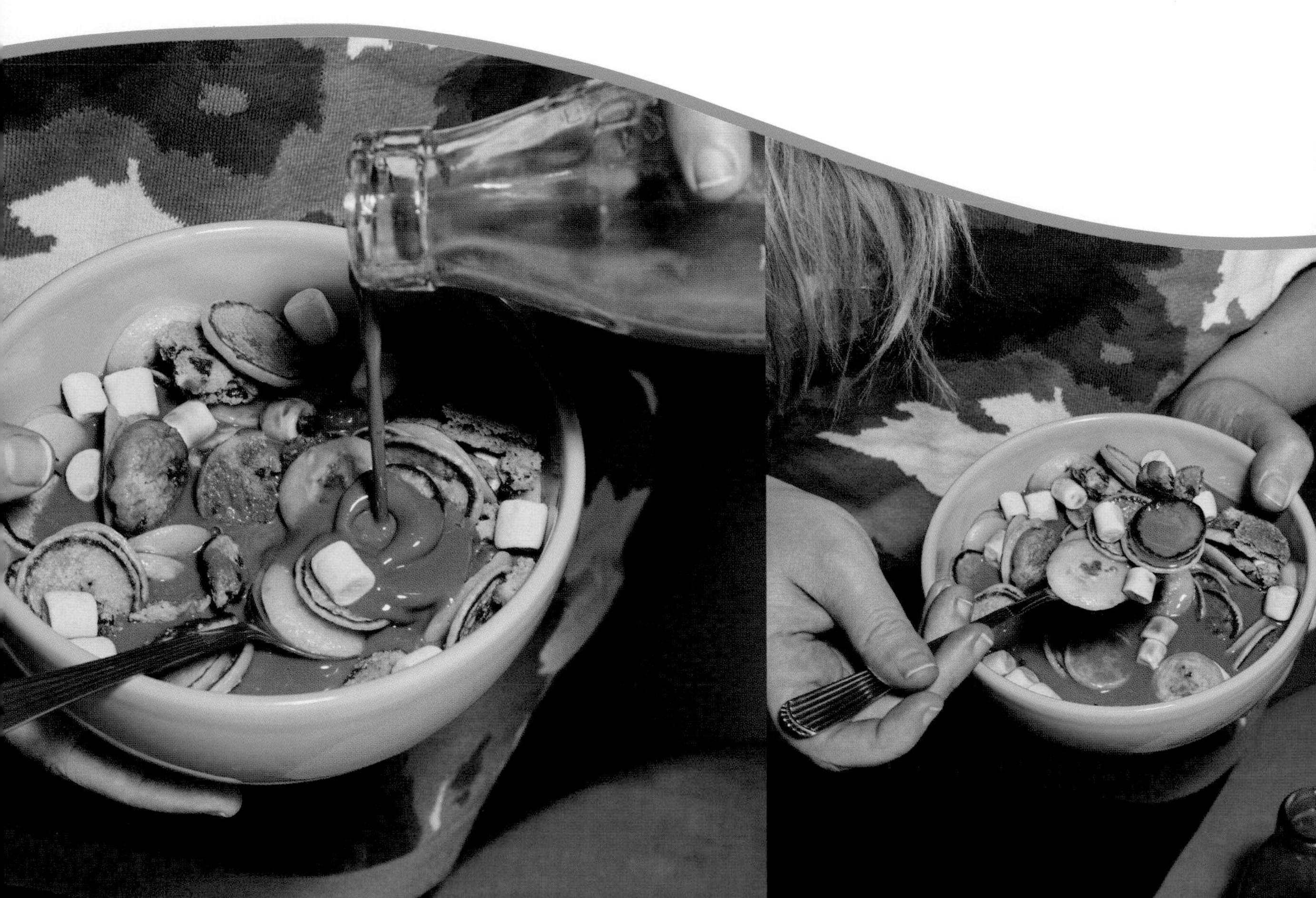

CHEESY CRUST BREAKFAST BURRITOS

PREP TIME: **10 MINUTES**
COOK TIME: **15 MINUTES**
DIFFICULTY: **MEDIUM**
SERVES: **2**
VEGETARIAN

Dropping Tex-Mex flavor bombs all over your brekkie. Roll this bad boy tortilla in a spicy cheese crust and douse in hot sauce, if you dare...

INGREDIENTS

1 (8–ounce [224–g]) can barbecue–flavored baked beans, or regular baked beans

1 ripe avocado

juice of ½ lime

1 teaspoon salted butter

3 eggs, lightly beaten

2 flour tortillas

2½ cups (250 g) grated Cheddar cheese

2 green chiles, deseeded and finely sliced

cilantro, roughly chopped

salt and pepper

hot sauce, to serve, (optional)

METHOD

1. Heat the baked beans in a saucepan over medium–low heat for 4-5 minutes, or in a microwave for 2½ minutes on high.
2. Meanwhile, lightly mash the avocado in a small bowl, then squeeze over the lime juice and season with salt. Stir to combine and set aside.
3. Melt the butter in a large frying pan over low heat and pour in the eggs. Once the eggs start to cook on the bottom, use a spatula to gently stir and fold the mixture. When the majority of the egg mixture is cooked, with a loose consistency, season with salt and pepper, then remove from the heat and set aside. The eggs will continue cooking a little, off the heat.
4. Transfer the eggs to a plate, clean the frying pan and return to medium heat. Gently warm the tortillas in the pan for 1 minute to soften, then remove and place on a cutting board.
5. Spread the avocado across the bottom half of the tortillas and top each one with scrambled egg, baked beans and ⅓ cup (35 g) of the cheese. Tightly roll the tortillas into burritos, starting from the base and folding in the sides as you roll to seal the edges.
6. Return the frying pan to medium–low heat. Add half the sliced green chiles to the middle of the pan and scatter over half the remaining cheese. Once the cheese is melted and starting to turn golden, place a burrito in the pan and carefully roll it up in the cheese crust. Repeat this step with the remaining green chiles, cheese and burrito.
7. Slice the burritos in half to reveal their layered fillings, then scatter with cilantro and serve with hot sauce, if you like.

PREP TIME: **5 MINUTES**
COOK TIME: **10 MINUTES**
DIFFICULTY: **EASY**
SERVES: **4**
MEAT

BACON EGG CUPS

Throw out your egg cups for these CRISPY BACON egg cups. Make sure you've got your buttery toast sticks for dunking in that oooooozy egg goodness.

INGREDIENTS

8 bacon slices
4 eggs
salt and pepper
4 slices buttered toast, sliced into sticks for dipping, to serve (optional)

METHOD

1. Preheat the broiler to high.
2. Wrap 4 of the bacon slices around the inside edges of 4 muffin molds and cut the other 4 slices in half so that you have 8 shorter slices of bacon. Criss-cross these over the bases of the muffin molds to form cups.
3. Broil the cups for 5 minutes, or until the bacon is cooked through but not crisp.
4. Crack an egg into each bacon cup and return to the broiler for 5 minutes, or until the egg has set.
5. Season with salt and pepper and enjoy with toast for dipping, if you like.

CHEESY CRUMPET LOAF

PREP TIME: **10 MINUTES**
COOK TIME: **30 MINUTES**
DIFFICULTY: **EASY**
SERVES: **4**
VEGAN

Crumpets don't need to just be crumpets. Elevate the ting, chuck in some vegan cheese and bake it so you can tear and share with the mandem.

INGREDIENTS

6 tablespoons (84 g) vegan non-dairy spread, softened
4 teaspoons yeast extract spread, such as Marmite
8 crumpets
2 cups (200 g) grated vegan Cheddar-style cheese

METHOD

1. Preheat the oven to 350°F (180°C, or gas mark 4) and line a loaf pan with parchment paper.
2. Whisk the softened non-dairy spread with the yeast extract spread in a small bowl until fully combined.
3. Top the crumpets with this mixture, then divide ⅓ cup (35 g) of the vegan cheese among them. Pile all the crumpets on top of each other and carefully transfer to the prepared loaf pan.
4. Sprinkle over the remaining vegan cheese and bake for 30 minutes until golden and bubbling.
5. Allow to cool for a few minutes before serving.

GLAZED DOUGHNUT BREAKFAST SANDOS

PREP TIME: **5 MINUTES**
COOK TIME: **15 MINUTES**
DIFFICULTY: **EASY**
SERVES: **2**
MEAT

Listen, don't you dare @ us until you actually try this. If using doughnuts for buns is wrong, then lock me up and throw away the key.

INGREDIENTS

4 smoked bacon slices
2 small burger patties
2 eggs
2 slices cheese
2 glazed doughnuts

METHOD

1. Preheat the broiler to high and lay the bacon and burger patties on a large foil-lined rimmed baking sheet. Broil for 5 minutes on each side until cooked through and starting to crisp up.
2. Remove the baking sheet from the broiler and crack in the eggs alongside the burgers and bacon. Return to the broiler and cook for 3–4 minutes, or until the eggs are cooked through. In the final minute, top the burgers with the cheese slices and allow to melt.
3. When ready to serve, slice the doughnuts in half horizontally and load them up with the cheesy burger patties, crispy bacon, and perfect broiled eggs. Serve immediately.

PREP TIME: **5 MINUTES**
COOK TIME: **5 MINUTES**
DIFFICULTY: **EASY**
SERVES: **2**
VEGAN

MAGIC SHELL BREAKFAST BOWLS

If breakfast's the most important meal of the day, you better make it a GOOD one. Whip up this magic brekkie bowl and smash the chocolate shell for a smoothie surprise!

INGREDIENTS

3 tablespoons coconut oil
8 ounces (224 g) frozen mixed berries
1 cup (240 g) vegan yogurt
5 tablespoons (75 ml) coconut milk (or any plant-based milk)
2 tablespoons hazelnut chocolate spread, such as Nutella
2 teaspoons chopped hazelnuts (optional)
2 tablespoons fresh raspberries (optional)

METHOD

1. Melt the coconut oil in a small saucepan over low heat and set aside to cool a little.
2. Put the frozen berries, yogurt and coconut milk in a food processor or high-powered blender and purée until smooth and thick. Cover and set aside in the refrigerator.
3. Stir the hazelnut chocolate spread into the melted coconut oil until fully combined.
4. Divide the thick smoothie mixture between 2 cereal bowls and pour over the melted chocolate mix. This should almost instantly set to a hard shell.
5. Top with chopped hazelnuts and raspberries, if you like, and dig in!

TIP:
Try swapping chocolate spread for speculoos spread and thank us later.

HONEY-NUT FRENCH TOAST

PREP TIME: **10 MINUTES**
COOK TIME: **10 MINUTES**
DIFFICULTY: **EASY**
SERVES: **2**
VEGETARIAN

I see your French toast and I raise you HONEY-NUT French toast. Eggy cinnamon-soaked brioche with a sweet honey-nut crunch coat. Yes.

INGREDIENTS

1 cup (50 g) honey–nut flake cereal
2 eggs, lightly beaten
½ cup (120 ml) milk
½ teaspoon ground cinnamon
4 brioche slices
2 tablespoons salted butter
2 tablespoons maple syrup, to serve (optional)

METHOD

1. Measure the cereal into a bowl and lightly crush with a rolling pin.
2. Combine the eggs, milk and cinnamon in a separate wide, shallow bowl.
3. Dip the slices of brioche into the egg mixture and turn to coat, then coat in the crushed cereal.
4. Melt the butter in a large frying pan over medium heat and gently fry the brioche slices for 3–5 minutes on each side until golden and crisp.
5. Serve with maple syrup.

CAUGHT LUNCHIN'

FOOD-WASTE HACKS

Don't be a WASTEMAN; save your leftover tings and whip them up into something beautiful.

BREADCRUMBS

Put stale or leftover bread, crusts and all, in a food processor and pulse into fine crumbs. These can be stored in the freezer for up to 3 months and can be used to coat chicken, fish and vegetables, or to thicken sauces. To use as a coating, defrost the crumbs, then spread them on a baking sheet and toast in the oven at 350°F (180°C, or gas mark 4), for 6–8 minutes until golden.

CHEESE RIND "STOCK CUBE"

You know you a bougie chefileeni when you find a Parmesan rind at the back of the refrigerator. Or maybe you're a basic-b chef with a stale block of Cheddar back there: you know, the one that escaped the plastic wrap? Whatever it is, we got you. Just throw this in with your tomato sauce ingredients (see page 15) to add FLAVORS and all-important sodium. You won't regret it.

HERBS FOR DAYZ

Found some rogue herbs chilling at the back of the refrigerator? Chop and freeze them (an ice-cube tray makes a great container), then add them to sauces as and when needed. Alternatively, add the herbs, stalks 'n' all, to your bottle of olive oil for a chefileeni infusion!

– BREAD –

CHILI CHEESE CROUTONS

PREP TIME: **5 MINUTES**

COOK TIME: **6–8 MINUTES**

DIFFICULTY: **EASY**

SERVES: **4 as a snack or salad or soup topping**

VEGETARIAN

INGREDIENTS

4 slices leftover or stale bread
3 tablespoons olive oil
1 teaspoon paprika
1 teaspoon sea salt
2 tablespoons finely grated Cheddar cheese

METHOD

1. Preheat the oven to 350°F (180°C, or gas mark 4). Line a baking sheet with parchment paper.
2. Slice the bread into bite-sized chunks and put them in a medium-sized bowl with the olive oil, paprika and salt. Toss everything together until the bread is well coated.
3. Spread the croutons on the prepared baking sheet and sprinkle over the Cheddar.
4. Bake for 6–8 minutes until golden, crisp and melted. Perfect added to a salad, or just as a snack. Enjoy!

– BREAD –

CINNAMON SHUGZ FRENCH TOAST BITES

PREP TIME: **5 MINUTES**

COOK TIME: **4 MINUTES**

DIFFICULTY: **EASY**

SERVES: **4 as a snack**

VEGETARIAN

INGREDIENTS

4 slices leftover or stale bread
1 egg
2 tablespoons whole milk
½ teaspoon vanilla extract
2 teaspoons sugar
½ teaspoon ground cinnamon
1 tablespoon unsalted butter

METHOD

1. Stack up the slices of bread and slice them into squares or cubes.
2. Whisk the egg, milk and vanilla together in a medium bowl.
3. Combine the sugar and cinnamon in a separate shallow bowl.
4. Dip the bread slices in the egg mixture, ensuring they are well coated. Allow any excess egg mixture to drip off, then turn the bread in the cinnamon sugar.
5. Melt the butter in a frying pan and fry the bites for 2 minutes on each side until golden and lightly toasted. Enjoy as they are, or dipped in melted chocolate.

JUICE CUBES

Got a load of half lemons and/or limes knocking around the refrigerator? Squeeze the juice into an ice-cube tray, freeze and save for future cocktails and salad dressings!

BANANA PEEL PURÉE

Got spare banaynays chilling in the fruit bowl? Next time you make banana bread, try this madness: Save the peels (trust), put them in a saucepan and cover with water. Bring to a gentle simmer and simmer for 20 minutes. Drain and rinse the peels under cold running water to cool them down, then purée until smooth in a food processor. Add the purée to your banana bread batter for a denser and all-round banging loaf!

Don't be a WASTEMAN

LEMONS & LIMES

CANDIED PEEL

PREP TIME: **10 MINUTES**

COOK TIME: **30 MINUTES**

DIFFICULTY: **EASY**

MAKES: **A SMALL BOWL**

VEGAN

INGREDIENTS

2 unwaxed lemons or limes

2 cups (480 ml) water

¾ cup (150 g) sugar

METHOD

1. Use a peeler to remove the zest from the lemons, then finely slice the zest into strips with a sharp knife.
2. Put the lemon zest in a small saucepan, then add the water and ½ cup (100 g) of the sugar and bring to a gentle simmer. Simmer for 30 minutes, then drain through a sieve.
3. Pat the peel dry with paper towels and toss in the remaining sugar. Store in an airtight container for up to 2 weeks and use to garnish cakes and cocktails.

APPLES

APPLE PEEL VODKA SOUR

PREP TIME: **5 MINUTES + 3–5 DAYS INFUSING**

COOK TIME: **NONE**

DIFFICULTY: **EASY**

MAKES: **700 ml BOTTLE**

VEGAN

INGREDIENTS

6 apples, peel only (we recommend Granny Smith or cooking apples)

juice of ½ lemon

¼ cup (50 g) sugar

700 ml bottle of vodka

METHOD

1. Put the apple peel, lemon juice and sugar in a large airtight storage jar and top with the vodka. Seal the jar and store in the refrigerator for 3–5 days to infuse.
2. Strain the vodka into a bottle. Store in a cool, dry place. Enjoy on its own or with a mixer of your choice for a totally bougie apple cocktail.

PESTO BAKED EGGS

PREP TIME: **5 MINUTES**
COOK TIME: **12 MINUTES**
DIFFICULTY: **EASY**
SERVES: **2**
VEGETARIAN

For when you want something EASY and delicious. Lazy days and that. Dunk a hunk of bread in these sensational pesto baked eggs and RELAX.

INGREDIENTS

½ cup (50 g) grated mozzarella cheese

2 tablespoons vegetarian green pesto

2 eggs

salt and pepper

½ teaspoon red pepper flakes

2 thick sourdough bread slices

2 tablespoons olive oil

METHOD

1. Preheat the oven to 350°F (180°C, or gas mark 4).
2. Divide the grated mozzarella between 2 ovenproof ramekins and top with the green pesto, then crack an egg into each. Season with salt, pepper and the red pepper flakes and bake in the oven for 12 minutes, or until the egg is cooked with a runny yolk.
3. Meanwhile, brush the sourdough with olive oil and toast in a frying pan for 2 minutes on each side over a medium–high heat. Season the toasted sourdough and slice into sticks.
4. Serve the baked pesto eggs, hot out of the oven, with the sourdough sticks for dipping.

ONE-PAN BLT PASTA SALAD

PREP TIME: **10 MINUTES**
COOK TIME: **15 MINUTES**
DIFFICULTY: **EASY**
SERVES: **4**
MEAT

When bacon, lettuce and tomato pair up with creamy, cheesy pasta, you better know you're in for a treat!

INGREDIENTS

2 cups (160 g) bacon lardons
1¾ cups (420 ml) whole milk
5 ounces (150 g) farfalle pasta
salt and pepper
¼ cup (25 g) finely grated Parmesan cheese
⅔ cup (160 ml) heavy cream
1⅓ cups (200 g) cherry tomatoes, halved
1 head romaine lettuce, sliced
1 tablespoon chopped parsley leaves
pinch of cayenne pepper

METHOD

1. Fry the bacon lardons in a large, deep frying pan with a well-fitting lid over medium-high heat until crisp. Remove the lardons from the pan and set aside on paper towels to drain the excess fat.
2. Add the milk and pasta to the same pan and season with salt and pepper. Bring to a boil over medium-high heat. Reduce the heat, cover and simmer for 10 minutes, until the pasta is cooked al dente and the liquid has thickened and been mostly absorbed. Remove the pan from the heat.
3. Stir in the Parmesan and heavy cream until the pasta is well coated. Add the drained bacon lardons, cherry tomatoes, lettuce and parsley and stir until evenly combined.
4. Divide among 4 warmed bowls and season each with a pinch of cayenne pepper.

PREP TIME: **10 MINUTES**
COOK TIME: **NONE**
DIFFICULTY: **EASY**
SERVES: **2**
FISH

BLOODY MARY SHRIMP COCKTAIL CUPS

The classic shrimp cocktail with a shot of vodka to put hairs on your chest. Who needs a bowl when nature gave us leaves?

INGREDIENTS

6 tablespoons (90 g) mayonnaise

1 tablespoon ketchup

2 teaspoons Tabasco sauce

½ teaspoon Worcestershire sauce

1 tablespoon vodka

juice of ½ lemon

¼ teaspoon salt

10 ounces (280 g) cooked jumbo shrimp

12 large leaves Baby Gem lettuce

pinch of cayenne pepper

dill sprigs and lemon slices, to serve (optional)

METHOD

1. In a large bowl, combine the mayonnaise, ketchup, Tabasco, Worcestershire sauce, vodka, lemon juice and salt. Add the shrimp and stir, ensuring they are evenly coated.
2. Spoon the shrimp mixture into the lettuce leaves and top with cayenne pepper, then serve with dill and lemon slices, if you like.

IN DA CLUB SANDWICH

PREP TIME: **15 MINUTES**
COOK TIME: **12 MINUTES**
DIFFICULTY: **EASY**
SERVES: **2**
VEGETARIAN

The Caught club sando is a STAPLE in the Caught Snackin' gang.

INGREDIENTS

6 white bread slices

9 tablespoons mayonnaise

1 tablespoon mustard (Dijon, or whole-grain)

salt and pepper

¼ head lettuce

2 large tomatoes, sliced

4 Cheddar cheese slices

1 large avocado, sliced

1 (1-ounce [28-g]) bag salt and vinegar or salted potato chips, plus more to serve (optional)

2 hard-boiled eggs, peeled and sliced

METHOD

1. Spread both sides of each slice of bread with mayonnaise, using 1 tablespoon for each slice, and lightly toast in a frying or griddle pan for 2 minutes on each side.
2. Combine the remaining 3 tablespoons of mayonnaise with the mustard in a small bowl.
3. Now construct the club sandwiches, seasoning with salt and pepper as you build. Top 2 slices of toasted bread with the mustard mayonnaise, lettuce, sliced tomatoes and Cheddar cheese slices.
4. Now top each one with another slice of toasted bread, followed by the sliced avocado, a small handful of potato chips and a sliced egg.
5. Top with the final slices of toasted bread and cut the sandwiches into quarters on the diagonal.
6. Skewer cocktail sticks through the sandwich quarters to hold them in place and serve with extra potato chips on the side, if you like.

QUICK CAULIFLOWER MAC & CHEESE

PREP TIME: **10 MINUTES + COOLING**

COOK TIME: **30 MINUTES**

DIFFICULTY: **EASY**

SERVES: **2**

VEGAN

The scrumptious lovechild of cauliflower 'n' cheese and macaroni 'n' cheese, topped with a crispy crumb. P.S., it's VEGAN.

INGREDIENTS

1¾ cups (420 ml) full-fat oat milk

½ head cauliflower, cut into small florets

1 bay leaf

salt and pepper

5 ounces (150 g) macaroni

1 tablespoon olive oil

2 cups (200 g) grated Cheddar-style vegan cheese

½ tablespoon mustard

2 handfuls cheese-flavored tortilla chips, crushed into fine crumbs

METHOD

1. Pour the oat milk into a large, deep frying pan with a well-fitting lid. Bring to a simmer over medium heat. Add the cauliflower florets and bay leaf and season with salt and pepper. Cover and allow to poach for 20 minutes, until the cauliflower is cooked through.
2. Meanwhile, bring a pan of salted water to a boil and cook the macaroni for 8 minutes. Drain and stir in the olive oil to stop the pasta from sticking together.
3. Remove the cauliflower pan from the heat and allow to cool. Discard the bay leaf, then blend the cauliflower mixture in a food processor, or use a stick blender, until you have a thickened, creamy sauce.
4. Return the sauce to the pan and gently heat. Add the grated vegan cheese and mustard and stir until the cheese has melted. Add the cooked pasta and stir to combine, ensuring it is well coated in the sauce.
5. Preheat the broiler to medium-high and transfer the contents of the pan to an ovenproof dish.
6. Top with the crumbled tortilla chips and place under the broiler for 8-10 minutes, until golden on top. Dig in.

PREP TIME: **10 MINUTES**
COOK TIME: **18 MINUTES**
DIFFICULTY: **EASY**
SERVES: **2**
MEAT

CHEESEBURGER CRUNCH WRAP

Juicy cheeseburger fillings wrapped snug in a fluffy tortilla, with a secret ingredient to bring that CRUNCH.

INGREDIENTS

2 burger patties
4 bacon slices
2 burger cheese slices
2 large flour tortillas
2 tablespoons burger sauce (see page 185)
4 iceberg lettuce leaves, sliced
½ large tomato, sliced
2 large pickles, sliced
12 plain or cheese-flavored tortilla chips
2 small flour tortillas

METHOD

1. Fry the burger patties and bacon in a large frying pan, set over medium-high heat, for 5-6 minutes on each side until golden-brown and cooked through. Remove from the heat and top the hot burgers with the cheese slices.
2. Spread the large tortillas with the burger sauce and construct the crunch wraps, starting with sliced iceberg lettuce, sliced tomato and the cooked cheeseburgers. Add the crispy bacon and sliced pickles, then top each crunch wrap with 6 tortilla chips arranged in a circle, like a wheel.
3. Place a small tortilla over the top of each one, then fold the larger, base tortillas up and over the smaller ones to seal the crunch wraps.
4. Fry the crunch wraps in the same large frying pan (one at a time) over medium-high heat for 2-3 minutes on each side until golden brown.
5. Cut the wraps in half to reveal their layers and dig in.

SHEET-PAN TOMATO SOUP

PREP TIME: **10 MINUTES + COOLING**

COOK TIME: **40 MINUTES**

DIFFICULTY: **EASY**

SERVES: **4**

VEGETARIAN

Good soup. (If you know, you know.)

INGREDIENTS

3 pounds (1.4 kg) cherry tomatoes

2 red chiles

2 garlic bulbs, halved horizontally

2 red onions, halved

2–3 thyme sprigs

2 bunches basil, plus baby leaves to serve (optional)

2 tablespoons olive oil

salt and pepper

1¼ cups (300 ml) vegetable stock, at room temperature

½ cup (120 g) crème fraîche

crusty bread, to serve (optional)

METHOD

1. Preheat the oven to 350°F (180°C, or gas mark 4).
2. Put the tomatoes, chilies, garlic and onions in a large roasting pan and top with the thyme, basil, olive oil and a generous pinch of salt and pepper.
3. Transfer to the oven and roast for 40 minutes, or until the tomato skins have become wrinkled and slightly charred. Remove from the oven and allow the vegetables to cool to room temperature, then squeeze the garlic cloves from their skins and discard the skins, along with the thyme sprigs.
4. Put the cooled vegetables into a food processor, along with the stock and crème fraîche, and purée until smooth. Alternatively, use a bowl and a stick blender.
5. Pour the soup into a deep saucepan over medium heat and warm through.
6. Season to taste and divide among 4 warmed bowls, topped with baby basil leaves and a thick slice of crusty bread, if you like.

PREP TIME: **10 MINUTES**
COOK TIME: **10 MINUTES**
DIFFICULTY: **EASY**
SERVES: **2**
VEGETARIAN

PIZZA TOASTIE

This pizza toastie is oozing with cheese and tomato sauce. Feel free to do a little freestyle and play around with the fillings and that... Experimentation, you get me?

INGREDIENTS

4 white bread slices
2 tablespoons (28 g) salted butter
8 tablespoons tomato pizza sauce (or see page 15)
2 cups (240 g) grated mozzarella cheese
1 large tomato, sliced
salt and pepper
4 tablespoons finely grated vegetarian Parmesan cheese
small handful of basil leaves

METHOD

1. Spread the slices of bread with the butter. Flip over 2 of the slices and spread with half the pizza sauce, then top with half the mozzarella cheese. Add the sliced tomato and season with salt and pepper, then scatter over 2 tablespoons of the Parmesan and half of the basil.
2. Top with the remaining slices of bread, buttered-sides up, and fry in an ovenproof pan over medium-high heat for 2 minutes.
3. Meanwhile, preheat the broiler to high.
4. Flip the toasties and spoon over the remaining pizza sauce, mozzarella and Parmesan and sprinkle on the rest of the basil.
5. Transfer the frying pan to the broiler for 5 minutes, until the toasties are golden and bubbling.
6. Allow to cool slightly before serving.

Oozing with cheese and tomato sauce

KIM-CHEESE SPRING ROLLS

PREP TIME: **25 MINUTES**
COOK TIME: **10 MINUTES**
DIFFICULTY: **MEDIUM**
SERVES: **4 (MAKES 8)**
VEGAN

The combo of kimchi and cheese in these DIY spring rolls BANGS! Eat hot and crispy straight from the pan with a spicy sriracha drizzle.

INGREDIENTS

1 (3-ounce [84-g]) package vegetable-flavor instant noodles plus it's seasoning sachet

1 cup (100 g) grated vegan cheese

16 rice paper sheets

2 cups (60 g) spinach leaves

1 (10-ounce [300-g]) jar kimchi

4 cups (960 ml) vegetable oil, for deep-frying

sriracha, to serve

TIP:
We double-wrap these bois to keep the filling intact while increasing all-important crunch levels.

METHOD

1. Cook the instant noodles according to the package instructions. Stir half the vegan cheese into the noodles while they're still hot.
2. Construct the spring rolls, one by one. Dip a sheet of rice paper in room-temperature water and lay on a clean surface. Lay a handful of spinach leaves horizontally across the center of the sheet and top with a spoonful of kimchi, then add an eighth of the cooked noodles and top with a generous sprinkling of cheese.
3. Lift the edge of the rice paper nearest to you over the filling and roll up tightly, tucking in the sides as you go to seal. Once rolled, wet another rice paper sheet and double-wrap the spring roll. Place on a wire rack while you construct the remaining spring rolls.
4. Heat the oil, in a deep saucepan with a well-fitting lid, to 350°F (180°C) and deep-fry the spring rolls, in 2 batches, for 2-3 minutes or until crispy and lightly golden. (See page 17 for deep-frying hacks.)
5. Place them on paper towels to drain off any excess oil.
6. Serve immediately with a bowl of sriracha sauce for dipping.

PREP TIME: **30 MINUTES + CHILLING**

COOK TIME: **15 MINUTES**

DIFFICULTY: **MEDIUM**

SERVES: **2–3**

FISH

ICE-CUBE TRAY SUSHI

People will be mind-blown at the shubz with this sushi ice-cube hack, trust me. Satisfying sushi bites topped with all ya favorite fishy flavors. Be sure to use rice vinegar here, as it's sweeter than regular vinegar.

INGREDIENTS

1 cup (250 g) sushi rice or sticky rice

1¼ cups (300 ml) cold water

1 teaspoon white rice vinegar

2 tablespoons vegetable oil

3½ ounces (100 g) smoked salmon

⅙ cucumber, peeled into ribbons and sliced into 2-inch (5-cm) lengths

6 cooked jumbo shrimp

1 avocado, halved, 1 half sliced, 1 half mashed

2 tablespoons sriracha mayonnaise

3 sheets salted seaweed, cut into fine ribbons with scissors

soy sauce, to serve

A mind-blowing sushi ice-cube hack, trust me

METHOD

1. Weigh the rice into a bowl, cover with cold water, then stir and drain. Repeat this process 3 times to wash the rice.
2. Put the washed rice in a medium-sized saucepan with a well-fitting lid and pour over the cold water. Cover with the lid and bring to a gentle simmer over medium-low heat. This should take about 10 minutes. Once simmering (you will hear it gently bubbling), avoid removing the lid. Reduce the heat to low for 5 minutes, then turn off the heat and set aside, lid on, for 15 minutes.
3. Transfer the cooked rice to a large baking sheet. Sprinkle over the vinegar and gently mix, then spread it out into a thin layer with a spatula. This will help the rice cool quickly.
4. When the rice is cool, start making the sushi. Lightly oil your ice-cube tray/s. Add slices of smoked salmon to 6 of the ice-cube compartments, cucumber to the next 6, a shrimp to each of the next 6 and sliced avocado to the final 6 compartments.
5. Spoon the sushi rice into each compartment and press it down with a spatula. Cover the tray/s and chill in the refrigerator for at least 20 minutes until the rice is firm.
6. When ready to serve, turn the sushi out onto a board or plate and top with spoonfuls of mashed avocado, sriracha mayo or shredded seaweed. Serve with soy sauce for dipping.

ONE-POT STICKY COLA WINGS

PREP TIME: **5 MINUTES**
COOK TIME: **45 MINUTES**
DIFFICULTY: **EASY**
SERVES: **4**
MEAT

These wings are gonna be a bit of a sticky sitch. Still, cola-infused for the win, and a sweet way to upgrade your basic wings.

INGREDIENTS

3 tablespoons (45 ml) vegetable oil
2 pounds (910 g) chicken wings
1 teaspoon salt
2 cups (480 ml) regular cola (not diet)
2 tablespoons soy sauce
2 star anise
1 tablespoon finely chopped garlic
2 scallions, sliced
1 teaspoon white sesame seeds
2 cups (250 g) sticky rice or Asian-style slaw, to serve (optional)

METHOD

1. Heat the vegetable oil in a large, deep frying pan with a well-fitting lid over medium-high heat.
2. Pat dry the chicken wings with paper towels and prick each one 4-5 times with a cocktail stick or skewer. Season with the salt and fry the wings, in batches, for 5 minutes on each side until golden and starting to crisp up.
3. Return all of the wings to the pan. Reduce the heat and pour in the cola and soy sauce, along with the star anise and garlic. Cover with the lid and simmer for 15 minutes.
4. Remove the lid and increase the heat to reduce the cola liquid to a sweet and sticky sauce. This should take about 10 minutes.
5. Once the sauce has reduced and coats the wings nicely, remove from the heat and serve on plates, topped with scallions and sesame seeds. Serve with sticky rice or Asian-style slaw, if you like.

PREP TIME: **10 MINUTES**
COOK TIME: **10 MINUTES**
DIFFICULTY: **EASY**
SERVES: **2**
VEGETARIAN

INSTANT NOODZ MAYO MAKEOVER

Everyone deserves a glow-up, no? Even instant noodz... give them a little contour and witness the flavors and vibes TAKE OFF!

INGREDIENTS

4 eggs

2 (3-ounce) packages vegetable-flavor instant noodles plus their seasoning sachets

2 garlic cloves, very finely chopped

2 tablespoons mayonnaise

1 teaspoon soy sauce

1 scallion, sliced

1 teaspoon mixed sesame seeds

METHOD

1. Bring a saucepan of water to a boil. Add 2 of the eggs and cook for 7 minutes, then remove with a slotted spoon and put the eggs in a bowl of cold water. Do not drain the boiling water. Once cool enough to handle, carefully peel the eggs and set aside.
2. Cook the noodles, without their seasoning sachets, in the reserved boiling water for 3 minutes. Reserve 2–3 tablespoons of the noodle water in a small bowl, then drain the noodles.
3. In a separate, large bowl, lightly beat the remaining 2 eggs with the contents of the seasoning sachets, along with the garlic, mayonnaise and soy sauce. Add the reserved noodle water, 1 tablespoon at a time, and whisk to combine. Add the noodles and fold them in the sauce until evenly coated.
4. Divide the noodles between 2 warmed bowls and top with the soft-boiled eggs, sliced in half to reveal their soft yolks. Scatter over the scallions and sesame seeds and serve.

FISH STICK TACOS

PREP TIME: **15 MINUTES**
COOK TIME: **15 MINUTES**
DIFFICULTY: **EASY**
SERVES: **2**
FISH

Don't know what to do with the fish sticks in your freezer? Level them up and try these tasty, tangy tacos with a citrus mango salsa.

INGREDIENTS

8 frozen fish sticks

½ mango, peeled, pitted and chopped

¼ red onion, sliced

1–2 jalapeños, deseeded and sliced

1 teaspoon chopped cilantro

juice of ½ lime

salt and pepper

4 small flour tortillas

2 large avocados, mashed

1 head Baby Gem lettuce, sliced

3 tablespoons sriracha mayonnaise

METHOD

1. Preheat the oven to 450°F (230°C, or gas mark 8). Lay the frozen fish sticks on a baking sheet and cook for 12–15 minutes.
2. Meanwhile, in a medium bowl, combine the mango, red onion, jalapeño(s), cilantro, lime juice and a pinch of salt and pepper to season.
3. Bend the tortillas in half to mimic a taco shell and place in the toaster. Toast for 2 minutes or until they crisp up and hold their shape.
4. Spoon the mashed avocado into the base of the tacos and top with sliced lettuce, 2 fish sticks per taco and a generous spoonful of mango salsa. Drizzle over sriracha mayonnaise and enjoy.

TIP:
We beg you to also try these with shrimp or langoustine..

CAULIFLOWER BASE PIZZA

PREP TIME: **10 MINUTES**
COOK TIME: **60 MINUTES**
DIFFICULTY: **EASY**
SERVES: **1–2**
VEGETARIAN

This no-dough pizza will have you shook when you try the crispy cauli base. Top with tomato sauce, melted cheese and colorful VEGETARIANs and bosh that nosh.

INGREDIENTS

1 small cauliflower, cut into florets

4 tablespoons olive oil

salt and pepper

¼ cup (25 g) finely grated vegetarian Parmesan cheese

2 cups (200 g) grated mozzarella cheese

1 egg

5 tablespoons (75 ml) tomato pizza sauce (or see page 15)

½ large tomato, sliced

¼ yellow pepper, sliced

½ cup (45 g) sliced cremini mushrooms

handful of basil leaves, to serve

METHOD

1. Preheat the oven to 325ºF (160ºC, or gas mark 3). Pulse the cauliflower in a food processor, until you have fine crumbs.
2. Transfer the cauliflower to a large baking sheet and spread it into a thin layer. Drizzle with 2 tablespoons of the olive oil and season with salt and pepper. Bake for 12–15 minutes until cooked through and pale golden.
3. Remove the cooked cauliflower from the oven and increase the oven temperature to 350°F (180°C, or gas mark 4).
4. When cool, pile the cooked cauliflower into a clean tea towel. Bring the corners of the towel over the top to seal and squeeze out any moisture over the sink.
5. In a large bowl, combine the cooked cauliflower with the Parmesan, half the mozzarella, the egg and 1 tablespoon of olive oil, and season with some salt and pepper. The mixture should come together into a thick dough.
6. Line the baking sheet with parchment paper. Transfer the cauliflower dough to the baking sheet, flattening and shaping it into a disk, roughly ½ inch (1 cm) thick.
7. Bake for 30 minutes, then top with the tomato sauce, the remaining mozzarella and the sliced vegetables. Drizzle with the remaining tablespoon of olive oil and season with salt and pepper. Bake for another 15 minutes. Serve, sliced and topped with basil leaves.

PREP TIME: **10 MINUTES**
COOK TIME: **5 MINUTES**
DIFFICULTY: **EASY**
SERVES: **2**
VEGAN

5-MINUTE CHILI OIL NOODLES

Slurp these thick udon noodz coated in spicy chili sauce and wait for your taste buds to take off! Made in five minutes, eaten in five seconds.

INGREDIENTS

5 ounces (140 g) thick udon noodles
1 tablespoon red pepper flakes
1 garlic clove, very finely chopped
1 tablespoon sesame oil
1 tablespoon chili oil
1 tablespoon mixed sesame seeds
1 tablespoon light soy sauce
3 tablespoons vegetable oil
salt and pepper

To serve (all optional)
steamed bok choy
1 scallion, sliced
1 red chile, finely chopped

METHOD

1. Cook the udon noodles according to the package instructions.
2. In a medium-large bowl, combine the red pepper flakes, garlic, sesame oil, chili oil, sesame seeds and soy sauce.
3. Heat the vegetable oil in a small saucepan over medium heat for 2 minutes, then pour this over the chili mixture and stir to combine.
4. Add the cooked noodles and stir until they are well coated. Serve in a bowl with steamed bok choy, sprinkled with scallions and red chile, if you like.

Slurp these thick udon noodz

CHEESY HOT DOG ROLLS

PREP TIME: **20 MINUTES**
COOK TIME: **20 MINUTES**
DIFFICULTY: **EASY**
SERVES: **2–4**
MEAT

If you want more rolls, look no further. A hot dog in sausage-roll camouflage, oozing with cheesy goodness and tangy mustard.

INGREDIENTS

1 sheet puff pastry

1 tablespoon all-purpose flour, to dust

4 tablespoons mustard

1 cup (100 g) grated Cheddar cheese

1 egg, lightly beaten

4 jumbo hot dogs

your favorite sauce, to serve

METHOD

1. Preheat the oven to 400°F (200°C, or gas mark 6).
2. Put the pastry sheet on a lightly floured surface and gently roll it out so it is about 1 inch (2.5 cm) longer and wider than its original size. Slice the sheet of puff pastry in half lengthwise, so you have 2 long rectangular sheets.
3. Leaving roughly ¾ inch (2 cm) along one of the long edges of each sheet bare, spread each pastry sheet with the mustard and top with the Cheddar. Brush the bare strip with the egg; this will act as a glue to seal the rolls.
4. Arrange the hot dogs (2 per sheet) lengthwise over the cheese and roll them up in the pastry, sealing them along the egg-brushed edge. You will have 2 large sausage rolls.
5. Slice the sausage rolls into bite-sized pieces, roughly 2 inches (5 cm) wide, and arrange them on a rimmed baking sheet. Brush with the remaining egg and bake in the oven for 20 minutes, until puffed and golden.
6. Serve with your favorite dipping sauce.

CORONATION TUNA MELT JACKETS

PREP TIME: **10 MINUTES**
COOK TIME: **20 MINUTES**
DIFFICULTY: **EASY**
SERVES: **4**
FISH

Why be basic with your potato jacket when you can turn up the flavors with a coronation drop? I'm talking spices, that sweet chutney and melty cheese VIBES!

INGREDIENTS

4 baking potatoes

1 (14-ounce [400-g]) can line-caught tuna

⅓ cup (80 g) mayonnaise

5 teaspoons mild curry powder

1 teaspoon ground turmeric

8 teaspoons mango chutney

2 scallions, sliced

salt and pepper

½ cup (50 g) grated Red Leicester or Cheddar cheese

To serve (all optional)

chopped cilantro

Greek yogurt

METHOD

1. Preheat the oven to 425°F (220°C, or gas mark 7).
2. Using a sharp knife, prick each potato 4–5 times; this will allow any steam to escape as it cooks. Microwave on high for 10 minutes, turning after 5 minutes. Allow to cool.
3. Meanwhile, in a medium-large bowl, combine the tuna, mayonnaise, curry powder, turmeric, half the mango chutney and the scallions. Season with salt and pepper.
4. With a sharp knife, carefully cut a large circle in the center of each potato and hollow out the fluffy filling. Add this to the tuna mixture.
5. Generously spoon the curried tuna-and-potato mixture into the jackets and top with the grated cheese. Place on a baking sheet and bake for 5–10 minutes until the cheese is melted and bubbling.
6. Serve the potatoes topped with the remaining mango chutney, along with some cilantro and a dollop of yogurt, if you like.

SPEEDY LASAGNA POCKETS

PREP TIME: **15 MINUTES**
COOK TIME: **20 MINUTES**
DIFFICULTY: **EASY**
SERVES: **4–6**
MEAT

Who wants to waste their sweet time whipping up a long-ass lasagna when you can make a speedy and sexy lasagna pocket?

INGREDIENTS

12 fresh lasagna sheets

1 pound (455 g) mozzarella slices

1 (14–ounce [400–g]) jar bechamel sauce

1 (12–ounce [350–g]) jar bolognese sauce

2½ cups (250 g) grated mozzarella cheese

olive oil

salt and pepper

basil leaves

mixed leaf salad, to serve (optional)

METHOD

1. Preheat the oven to 350°F (180°C, or gas mark 4) and line a baking sheet with parchment paper.
2. Lay the lasagna sheets across a deep baking pan. Boil some water and then pour over the lasagna sheets. Allow the sheets to soak for 2 minutes until softened.
3. Carefully remove the lasagna sheets from the hot water and place on a cutting board, stacked up in a neat pile. Using a sharp knife, trim roughly 1¼ inches (3 cm) off the long edge of each sheet, to make them a little thinner. This will make the folding process easier and will result in neater pockets.
4. Lay a lasagna sheet, vertically, on a board or plate and place a slice of mozzarella in the center. Top the mozzarella with a spoonful of creamy bechamel sauce.
5. Now add another lasagna sheet over the top, this time horizontally so it makes a cross shape with the first. Add another slice of mozzarella to the center of the second sheet, followed by a spoonful of the bolognese.
6. Starting with the bottom lasagna sheet, fold the bare edges up and over the bolognese. Finish with another spoonful of creamy bechamel sauce and a generous sprinkling of grated mozzarella. Repeat with the remaining ingredients.
7. Place the pockets on the prepared baking sheet, then drizzle with olive oil and season with salt and pepper. Bake for 20 minutes until golden and bubbling.
8. Top with basil leaves and serve, with a mixed leaf salad on the side, if you like.

CAUGHT PLAYLIST

Part of the prep is setting the vibes. Here are Spotify codes to 2 playlists we listen to while cooking. We will be updating them regularly.

Garage playlist

Vibes playlist

CAUGHT DININ'

DARK 'N' STORMY RIBS

PREP TIME: **10 MINUTES**
COOK TIME: **40 MINUTES**
DIFFICULTY: **EASY**
SERVES: **2–4**
MEAT

There are two Rs in life that matter: rum and ribs, in that order. This recipe will have you sweet, sticky and sensational ribs in an hour—yes, really. Hold tight, it's gonna get STORMY out there.

INGREDIENTS

2½- to 3-pound (1.2- to 1.4-kg) rack of pork ribs

2 tablespoons salt

6 cups (1440 ml) ginger beer

1 cup (200 g) soft dark brown sugar

1 cup (240 ml) dark rum

2 tablespoons soy sauce

2 teaspoons cayenne pepper

2 teaspoons garlic powder

½ teaspoon red pepper flakes

coleslaw and grilled corn cobettes, to serve (optional)

METHOD

1. Put the ribs in a large saucepan with 1 tablespoon of the salt and cover with 4 cups (960 ml) of the ginger beer. Bring to a gentle simmer over medium heat. Simmer for 30 minutes, skimming the froth off the top with a large spoon after 10 minutes.
2. Meanwhile, make the glaze. Combine ¾ cup (150 g) of the sugar with the remaining 2 cups (480 ml) ginger beer, the dark rum and the soy sauce in a large frying pan. Bring to a gentle simmer over medium-low heat. Simmer the sauce for 15 minutes, stirring occasionally, until it has reduced to a syrup-like consistency.
3. Remove from the heat and allow to cool for 10 minutes or so. The glaze will continue to thicken as it cools.
4. After 20 minutes, remove the ribs from the ginger beer, pouring this away.
5. Combine the remaining ¼ cup (50 g) sugar and remaining 1 tablespoon salt in a small bowl, along with the cayenne pepper, garlic powder and red pepper flakes. Rub this over the ribs and lay them across a wire rack with a baking sheet underneath.
6. Preheat the broiler to high and place the ribs underneath for 10 minutes, turning and brushing them generously with the glaze halfway through. The ribs will be sticky and caramelized.
7. Portion up the ribs and serve with any remaining glaze poured over, alongside some coleslaw and grilled corn cobettes, if you like.

PREP TIME: **10 MINUTES**
COOK TIME: **8 MINUTES**
DIFFICULTY: **MEDIUM**
SERVES: **2**
FISH

BANG BANG SHRIMP

If you're looking to flex on the mandem or impress the sweet ones, this will do it. Crunchy textures are on point, looking very chefileeni with this one…

INGREDIENTS

2 tablespoons mayonnaise

2 teaspoons sriracha

2 teaspoons sweet chili sauce

1 (3-ounce [84-g]) hot chili-flavored corn puffs

⅓ cup (40 g) panko breadcrumbs

⅓ cup (40 g) cornstarch

2 eggs, lightly beaten

6 ounces (180 g) raw jumbo shrimp

1 cup (240 ml) vegetable oil, for deep-frying

2 cups (250 g) sticky rice (optional)

1 scallion, sliced (optional)

METHOD

1. Combine the mayonnaise, sriracha and chili sauce in a small bowl and set aside. This is your bang bang sauce.
2. Put the chili-flavored corn puffs in a medium-sized bowl and gently crush into crumbs using a rolling pin. Add the panko breadcrumbs and stir until well combined. Put the cornstarch in a second bowl and the beaten egg in a third.
3. Pat dry the shrimp with paper towels, then coat in cornstarch, followed by the beaten egg and finally the chili-panko crumbs. Set aside on a plate.
4. Heat the oil to 350°F (180°C) in a frying pan with a well-fitting lid over medium heat and deep-fry the shrimp, in 2 batches, for 4 minutes on each side until evenly golden and crisp. Remove from the pan and drain on paper towels. (See page 17 for deep-frying hacks.)
5. Serve the shrimp with the bang bang sauce, on a bed of sticky rice and scattered with scallions, if you like.

TIP:
Double the cornstarch, egg and panko crumb mix and coat the shrimp twice for extra-crispy shrimp.

CREAMY VODKA PASTA

PREP TIME: **15 MINUTES**
COOK TIME: **15 MINUTES**
DIFFICULTY: **EASY**
SERVES: **4**
VEGETARIAN

Believe me when I tell you this sauce is so silky that it glistens... Rich, creamy and a little bit naughty with the voddy.

INGREDIENTS

1 onion, finely chopped

2 garlic cloves, very finely chopped

2 red chilies, deseeded and finely chopped

1 cup (240 ml) heavy cream

1 cup (240 ml) tomato purée

1 pound (455 g) spaghetti

4 cups (960 ml) water

¾ cup (60 g) finely grated vegetarian Parmesan cheese

2 tablespoons (30 ml) vodka

handful of basil leaves

salt and pepper

METHOD

1. Put the onion, garlic, chilies, cream, tomato purée, spaghetti and water into a large, deep frying pan with a well-fitting lid.
2. Cover and bring to a boil over medium-high heat, then reduce the heat to low and simmer for 12 minutes, or until the pasta is cooked and has absorbed some of the sauce.
3. Add the Parmesan and vodka and stir to combine, cooking for a further 2-3 minutes.
4. Divide among 4 warmed bowls and serve, topped with a handful of basil leaves. Season with salt and pepper.

ONE-POT-WONDER BAKED TOMATO RISOTTO

PREP TIME: **5 MINUTES**
COOK TIME: **1 HOUR**
DIFFICULTY: **EASY**
SERVES: **4**
VEGETARIAN

This boi really be a one-pot-WONDER when it's this darn tasty! The creamy baked feta melted with that tangy tomato sauce... Unbelievable scenes.

INGREDIENTS

5 cups (750 g) cherry tomatoes
1 (8-ounce [224-g]) block feta cheese
small bunch of basil
3 tablespoons olive oil, plus extra to serve
1¾ cups (300 g) arborio rice
¼ cup (60 ml) white wine
1½ cups (360 ml) vegetable stock
salt and pepper

METHOD

1. Preheat the oven to 350°F (180°C, or gas mark 4).
2. Pour the cherry tomatoes into an oven dish. Place the block of feta in the center. Add the basil, then drizzle with the 3 tablespoons of olive oil and season generously with salt and pepper. Bake for 25 minutes until the tomatoes are starting to caramelize and the feta has softened and melted slightly.
3. Remove the dish from the oven, discard the basil and mix the feta and tomatoes together to make a rich, creamy sauce.
4. Stir in the rice, wine and stock and return to the oven for 30-35 minutes, until the rice is cooked through and has expanded, absorbing the stock. Serve in warmed bowls.

PREP TIME: **5 MINUTES**
COOK TIME: **30 MINUTES**
DIFFICULTY: **EASY**
SERVES: **2**
VEGETARIAN

EASY PEKING FUN GUY PANCAKES

Be a fun guy with these shroom-packed Peking pancakes, finessed with a crunch from all them fresh VEGETARIANs.

INGREDIENTS

For the hoisin sauce

1 tablespoon sesame oil
3 tablespoons soy sauce
2 tablespoons rice wine vinegar
1 tablespoon sriracha
1 tablespoon honey

For the pancakes

8 large portobello mushrooms
8 Chinese pancakes
½ cucumber, deseeded and sliced into matchsticks
2 scallions, sliced into strips
2 teaspoons white sesame seeds

METHOD

1. Preheat the oven to 325°F (160°C, or gas mark 3).
2. Put all the hoisin sauce ingredients into a small bowl and stir to combine.
3. Arrange the mushrooms on a baking sheet and pour over the sauce, then bake for 30 minutes until cooked through and golden.
4. Remove from the oven and shred the mushrooms with 2 forks, mixing them with the sauce as you do so.
5. Transfer the mushrooms to a serving dish and serve alongside the other ingredients for people to build their pancakes themselves.
6. To construct the pancakes, simply add a spoonful of the mushrooms to a pancake and top with cucumber, scallions and a pinch of sesame seeds. Roll up and enjoy!

Be a fun guy with these shroom-packed pancakes

QUICK GNOCCHI WITH A GREEN CHEESE SAUCE

PREP TIME: **15 MINUTES**
COOK TIME: **15 MINUTES**
DIFFICULTY: **EASY**
SERVES: **2**
VEGETARIAN

Don't be shook! This easy DIY gnocchi will make you look like a top chefileeni. We won't tell anyone you used premade mashed potatoes—we got you.

INGREDIENTS

1½ cups (180 g) all-purpose flour, plus more to dust

½ teaspoon salt

1 (14-ounce [400-g]) package or leftover mashed potato

3 garlic cloves, very finely chopped

3 tablespoons (30 g) finely grated vegetarian Parmesan cheese

1 egg, lightly beaten

2½ tablespoons (35 g) unsalted butter

1 bunch of basil

1 cup (240 ml) whole milk

1½ cups (150 g) grated Cheddar cheese

pepper

¼ cup (30 g) toasted breadcrumbs (see page 88)

METHOD

1. Bring a large pan of salted water to a boil.
2. Meanwhile, put 1¼ cups (150 g) of the flour in a bowl with the salt, mashed potato, garlic, Parmesan and egg. Combine to make a dough. Transfer the dough to a floured surface. Knead the dough for no more than 1 minute until soft but smooth and holding its shape. Dust in a little more flour if the dough is too loose and sticky.
3. Divide the dough into quarters, rolling each into a long sausage about 1 inch (2.5 cm) thick. Cut the sausages into 1-inch (2.5-cm) pieces and boil for 5–6 minutes, or until the gnocchi start to float. Drain.
4. Melt 1 tablespoon (14 g) of the butter in a frying pan over medium heat and fry the drained gnocchi in batches for 2–3 minutes on each side.
5. Meanwhile, in a blender, blend the basil and ¼ cup (60 ml) of the milk until you have a vibrant green sauce.
6. Melt the remaining 1½ tablespoons (21 g) of butter in a saucepan over medium heat and whisk in the remaining ¼ cup (30 g) of flour. Cook for 2 minutes, whisking, until pale golden. Pour in the remaining ¾ cup (180 ml) milk, bit by bit, and whisk after each addition until you have a smooth sauce.
7. Cook the sauce for 2 minutes until thickened. Add the Cheddar, stirring, until rich and creamy. Stir in the basil mixture; this will turn the sauce a vibrant green. Taste and season with a little salt and pepper.
8. Serve the gnocchi with the green cheese sauce poured over and a generous sprinkle of toasted breadcrumbs.

PREP TIME: **10 MINUTES**
COOK TIME: **10 MINUTES**
DIFFICULTY: **EASY**
SERVES: **2**
VEGAN

10-MINUTE THAI GREEN CURRY

Fine Thai cuisine in 10 minutes? MADNESS. Blessed with health, thanks to all them VEGETARIANs.

INGREDIENTS

- 1 tablespoon coconut oil
- 2 garlic cloves, sliced
- 2 green Thai chilies, sliced
- ½ eggplant, cut into small cubes
- ¾ cup (100 g) baby corn
- ¾ cup (100 g) sugar snap peas
- 1 red pepper, sliced
- 1 (14-ounce [400-ml]) can coconut milk
- 2 tablespoons vegan Thai green curry paste
- 1 (8-ounce [224-g]) cooked Thai jasmine microwaveable rice pouch
- salt and pepper
- small handful of Thai basil leaves, or cilantro, to serve (optional)

METHOD

1. Melt the coconut oil in a large, deep frying pan, over medium-high heat. Add the garlic, chilies, eggplant, baby corn, sugar snap peas and red pepper. Fry for 2 minutes, stirring, until the vegetables have started to soften and brown a little.
2. Pour in the coconut milk and bring to a boil, then reduce the heat to a simmer.
3. Stir in the Thai green curry paste and simmer for 8 minutes.
4. Meanwhile, microwave the rice according to the package instructions.
5. Taste the curry and season with salt and pepper accordingly, then remove from the heat and stir in the Thai basil or cilantro, if using. Divide the jasmine rice and curry between warmed bowls and serve.

RUSTIC RAVIOLI LASAGNA

PREP TIME: **10 MINUTES**
COOK TIME: **25 MINUTES**
DIFFICULTY: **EASY**
SERVES: **4**
VEGETARIAN

This hot twist on lasagna is a banger! Why use basic-b pasta sheets when you can save time and increase flavors with ravioli layers?

INGREDIENTS

2 cups (480 ml) tomato pizza sauce (or see page 15)

1 pound (455 g) fresh vegetarian ravioli (such as butternut squash or mushroom filling)

18 mozzarella cheese slices

salt and pepper

drizzle of olive oil

METHOD

1. Preheat the oven to 375°F (190°C, or gas mark 5).
2. Pour one-third of the tomato sauce across the bottom of a large oven dish and top with one-third of the ravioli, in a single layer. Arrange 6 slices of mozzarella across the top and season with salt and pepper. Repeat this layering twice more.
3. Drizzle with olive oil and bake for 25 minutes, until golden and bubbling, then serve.

Save time and increase flavors with ravioli

PREP TIME: **15 MINUTES**
COOK TIME: **45 MINUTES**
DIFFICULTY: **MEDIUM**
SERVES: **2**
VEGAN

VEGETARIAN TIKKA MASALA NAAN BOWLS

Make yourself a fresh naan bowl filled with VEGETARIAN masala curry. Save the washing-up and feed your soul!

INGREDIENTS

For the naan bowls

1⅔ cups (200 g) self-rising flour

½ cup (120 g) Greek-style vegan yogurt, plus more as needed

salt and pepper

2 tablespoons olive oil, for brushing and drizzling

For the tikka masala

2 tablespoons vegetable oil

½ onion, finely chopped

2 garlic cloves, very finely chopped

1 teaspoon peeled and finely grated fresh ginger

2 red chilies, deseeded and sliced

1 teaspoon garam masala

½ teaspoon ground turmeric

2 sweet potatoes, peeled and cubed

1 green pepper, sliced

6 ounces (180 g) canned chickpeas (drained weight)

1½ cups (360 ml) canned coconut milk

2 tablespoons tomato purée

2 cups (250 g)cooked basmati rice and chopped cilantro, to serve (optional)

METHOD

1. Preheat the oven to 375°F (190°C, or gas mark 5).
2. Combine the flour and vegan yogurt in a mixing bowl, along with some salt and pepper, until you have a smooth dough. Wrap in plastic wrap and set aside to rest.
3. Meanwhile, heat the vegetable oil in a large, deep frying pan over medium heat. Sweat the onion, garlic, ginger and chilies with the garam masala and turmeric.
4. After about 10 minutes, add the sweet potatoes, green pepper and chickpeas, and cook for a further 5 minutes, stirring.
5. Pour in the coconut milk and tomato purée and stir to combine, then reduce the heat and simmer for 20 minutes.
6. Meanwhile, divide the rested dough into 4 balls and flatten each ball into a disk roughly ¼ inch (6 mm) thick. Brush 4 ovenproof bowls with olive oil and place a disk of dough inside each bowl. The bowls will act as a mold for the naans, shaping them as they bake.
7. Drizzle the dough with the remaining olive oil, season with salt and pepper and bake for 25–30 minutes until golden.
8. Remove the bowls from the oven and carefully turn out the naans. Spoon the tikka masala into the naan bowls. Top with cilantro and serve with basmati rice, if you like.

50-GARLIC CHICKEN KIEVS

PREP TIME: **15 MINUTES + COOLING + CHILLING**
COOK TIME: **65 MINUTES**
DIFFICULTY: **MEDIUM**
SERVES: **4**
MEAT

What's the most garlic you've ever seen in a recipe? Don't answer that, because we topped everyone with 50 cloves. YES, 50!

INGREDIENTS

5 small garlic bulbs

¼ cup (60 ml) olive oil

salt and pepper

2 cups (240 g) breadcrumbs (see page 88)

½ cup (120 g) salted butter, at room temperature

1 cup (30 g) chopped parsley leaves

1 cup (100 g) finely grated Parmesan cheese, or any other hard cheese

½ teaspoon red pepper flakes

4 large chicken breasts

½ cup (60 g) all-purpose flour

2 eggs, lightly beaten

french fries or mashed potatoes and steamed greens, to serve (optional)

METHOD

1. Preheat the oven to 350°F (180°C, or gas mark 4).
2. Slice the tops off the garlic bulbs and discard. Lay the bulbs on a sheet of foil, drizzle with the olive oil and season with salt and pepper. Bake for 35 minutes, until soft, golden and fragrant.
3. Meanwhile, spread the breadcrumbs on a baking sheet and toast in the oven for 8–10 minutes, or until pale golden. Set aside to cool. If toasting in advance, allow to cool and store in an airtight container.
4. When the garlic is out of the oven and has cooled enough to handle, squeeze the soft cloves from their skins into a medium-sized bowl (you should have about 50 cloves). Add the soft butter, chopped parsley, Parmesan and red pepper flakes, and season with salt and pepper. Stir or whisk until well combined and transfer to a piece of plastic wrap or parchment paper. Shape the flavored butter into a chunky cylinder and chill in the refrigerator for 20 minutes.
5. When the butter has hardened, slice it into 4 disks roughly ¾ inch (2 cm) thick. Using a sharp knife, slice into the chicken breasts along one side to create a pocket. Push a disk of garlic butter into each breast and press the pocket closed.
6. Put the flour, eggs and toasted breadcrumbs into 3 separate bowls.
7. Coat the chicken breasts in flour, then in egg and finally in breadcrumbs. Repeat the egg and breadcrumb steps to double-seal the chicken breasts. This will help stop the garlic butter from spilling out during baking and ensure your Kievs are extra crispy!
8. Lay the Kievs on a wire rack set over a baking sheet and bake for 25–30 minutes, or until cooked through. Serve with french fries or mashed potatoes and steamed greens, if you like.

Watch the pink POP in our magical rice bowl

UNICORN RICE BOWLS

PREP TIME: **10 MINUTES**
COOK TIME: **30 MINUTES**
DIFFICULTY: **EASY**
SERVES: **2**
VEGAN

Colors on colors! Squeeze lime over this rice and watch the pink POP in our magical rice bowl. Yes, with vegan cheese puffs... AND WHAT?

INGREDIENTS

⅔ cup (160 ml) white wine vinegar

1 tablespoon sugar

1 large carrot, peeled into ribbons

½ cucumber, peeled into ribbons

¼ red cabbage, finely sliced

1 cup (150 g) Thai sticky rice

juice of 1 lime

1 avocado, sliced

small handful of vegan cheese puffs

1 tablespoon vegan mayonnaise

2 tablespoons sriracha

2 tablespoons cilantro leaves, torn

½ teaspoon mixed sesame seeds

TIP:
Swap the rice for 8 ounces (224 g) vermicelli noodles to make mermaid hair bowls.

METHOD

1. Combine the white wine vinegar and sugar in a bowl, stirring until the sugar has dissolved. Add the carrot and cucumber ribbons, cover and set aside for 30 minutes to pickle.
2. Bring a saucepan of salted water to a boil and cook the red cabbage for 5 minutes. Strain the cabbage over a large measuring jug, reserving the blue cooking water.
3. Add the rice to the now-empty saucepan and pour over 1¼ cups (300 ml) of the blue cabbage water. Return the saucepan to the stove, over very low heat. Cover and cook for 25 minutes.
4. Once the rice is cooked and has turned purple, having absorbed all the colored water, spread it across a plate to cool.
5. Squeeze the lime juice over the cooled rice. The areas hit by the lime juice will turn a bright pink, giving the rice a purple-and-pink tie-dyed effect!
6. Now construct the unicorn bowls. Divide the rice between 2 bowls. Top each with a small handful of red cabbage. Drain and rinse the pickled vegetables ribbons under cold water, then arrange them around the edges of the bowls. Finish with the slices of avocado and a small handful of vegan cheese puffs for that all-important crunch!
7. In a small bowl, combine the vegan mayo and sriracha. Drizzle this over the bowls, then scatter over the cilantro and sesame seeds and serve.

PREP TIME: **10 MINUTES**
COOK TIME: **1 HOUR**
DIFFICULTY: **EASY**
SERVES: **4**
MEAT

CHEESY SHEPHERD'S PIE POTATO SKINS

You know we have to take a British classic and put that Snackin' finesse on it! Shepherd's pie loaded in crispy potato skins with lots of melted cheeeeese.

INGREDIENTS

4 large baking potatoes

2 tablespoons vegetable oil

½ onion, finely chopped

2 garlic cloves, very finely chopped

1 carrot, finely chopped

10 ounces (280 g) ground lamb

2 teaspoons Worcestershire sauce

salt and pepper

large handful of frozen peas

2 tablespoons (28 g) salted butter

½ cup (50 g) finely grated Cheddar cheese

1 (1-ounce [28-g]) bag cheese-flavored corn chips, crushed

steamed greens, to serve

METHOD

1. Preheat the oven to 375°F (190°C, or gas mark 5).
2. Using a sharp knife, prick each potato 4–5 times; this will allow any steam to escape during baking. Wrap the potatoes in foil and bake for 50 minutes, or simply microwave on high (without foil) for 10 minutes, turning after 5 minutes.
3. Meanwhile, heat the oil in a large frying pan over medium–low heat and sweat the onion, garlic and carrot until softened.
4. Increase the heat to medium–high and add the lamb, breaking it up with a wooden spoon as it cooks. Brown the lamb for 8–10 minutes, then add a splash of water, along with the Worcestershire sauce and some salt and pepper. Reduce the heat and gently simmer for 20 minutes.
5. Stir the frozen peas into the lamb mixture.
6. Remove the baked potatoes from the oven and slice in half. Spoon out their centers into a large mixing bowl. Combine the fluffy potato with the butter, Cheddar and a pinch of salt and pepper.
7. Spoon the lamb mixture into each potato skin. Top with the cheesy mash, then sprinkle over the crushed corn chips. Return to the oven for 10 minutes until golden on top.
8. Allow to cool a little before serving with a side of steamed greens.

FISH STICK KATSU CURRY

PREP TIME: **15 MINUTES**
COOK TIME: **15 MINUTES**
DIFFICULTY: **EASY**
SERVES: **2**
FISH

Need I say more? Flaky fish sticks finessed with that aromatic creamy katsu curry. Vibes for days.

INGREDIENTS

6 fish sticks

For the curry sauce

1 tablespoon vegetable oil
½ onion, finely chopped
2–3 carrots, diced
2 garlic cloves, very finely chopped
1 teaspoon peeled and finely grated fresh ginger
1 teaspoon garam masala
½ teaspoon ground turmeric
2 tablespoons honey
1 tablespoon soy sauce
1¾ cups (420 ml) vegetable stock
½ cup (120 g) jasmine rice
salt and pepper

To serve (all optional)

cilantro
sesame seeds
baby spinach leaves
Butterhead lettuce leaves
raw carrot ribbons

METHOD

1. Preheat the oven to 450°F (230°C, or gas mark 8). Place the fish sticks on a baking sheet and cook for 12 minutes.
2. Meanwhile, heat the oil in a frying pan over medium–low heat and sweat the onion, carrot, garlic and ginger with the garam masala and turmeric.
3. After 5 minutes, stir in the honey and soy sauce and pour over the stock. Increase the heat and bring the sauce to a boil, then reduce the heat and simmer for 10 minutes, or until the sauce has thickened. If you prefer a smoother sauce, use a stick blender to blend the sauce to a silky consistency. Taste and season accordingly.
4. Meanwhile, cook the rice according to the package instructions.
5. Serve the fish sticks with a mound of rice and the katsu curry sauce generously spooned over the top. Sprinkle with cilantro leaves and sesame seeds, if you like, or serve with a side salad for added color.

TIP:
Want a vegetarian option? See the Veggie Katsu Curry on page 177.

PREP TIME: **10 MINUTES**
COOK TIME: **45 MINUTES**
DIFFICULTY: **EASY**
SERVES: **4**
MEAT

TOAD-IN-THE-HOLE LOAF

Who needs plain old bread when you can have this BANGER in loaf form! British comfort food at its best.

INGREDIENTS

2 cups (240 g) all-purpose flour
2 teaspoons mustard powder
½ teaspoon salt
3 eggs
¾ cup (180 ml) whole milk
8 pork sausages
3 tablespoons (45 ml) vegetable oil
caramelized red onion gravy and mixed vegetables, to serve (optional)

METHOD

1. Preheat the oven to 425°F (220°C, or gas mark 7).
2. Sift the flour, mustard powder and salt into a large mixing bowl, then add the eggs and beat to combine. Once you have a smooth, thick mixture, gradually whisk in the milk until a loose batter forms. Cover and place in the refrigerator for 15 minutes to chill.
3. Meanwhile, lay the sausages along the bottom of a loaf pan and bake for 10 minutes until lightly browned.
4. Remove the loaf pan from the oven. Take out the sausages and set aside, then pour the vegetable oil into the pan and return to the oven for 3 minutes to heat the oil.
5. When the oil is hot, pour in the chilled batter and add the sausages; they will sink into the batter a little. Carefully return the pan to the oven for 30–35 minutes. Do not open the oven door during this time, or the batter may fail to rise, or collapse. After this time, the batter should have fluffed up with a golden crust and the sausages should be a deep golden brown.
6. Allow to cool a little, then turn out onto a board and slice into portions.
7. Serve with onion gravy and mixed vegetables for the perfect dinner!

CHEESE HAT CHILI

PREP TIME: **10 MINUTES**
COOK TIME: **30 MINUTES**
DIFFICULTY: **EASY**
SERVES: **4**
VEGAN

Cheeeeeeeese hat chili. Hearty sweet and potato flavaaas tucked underneath a crispy cheese hat.

INGREDIENTS

2 tablespoons olive oil
1 onion, finely chopped
2 garlic cloves, very finely chopped
1 large sweet potato, peeled and chopped
1 (14-ounce [400-g]) can chopped tomatoes
1¾ cups (420 ml) vegetable stock
1 (14-ounce [400-g]) can red kidney beans, drained
1 (14-ounce [400-g]) can black beans, drained
1 teaspoon chilli powder
1 teaspoon smoked paprika
1 teaspoon ground cumin
1 teaspoon cocoa powder
salt and pepper
2 cups (240 g) grated vegan cheese
2 jalapeños, sliced
long-grain rice, avocado and cilantro, to serve (optional)

METHOD

1. Heat the oil in a large, deep ovenproof frying pan over medium heat and sweat the onion, garlic and sweet potato.
2. Once the vegetables have started to soften (around 10 minutes), add the canned tomatoes, stock, beans, spices and cocoa, and season with salt and pepper. Stir to combine and simmer over low heat for 20 minutes until the sauce has reduced.
3. Preheat the broiler to medium.
4. Top the chili with the vegan cheese in a generous layer and scatter over the sliced jalapeños. Place under the broiler for 10 minutes, until the cheese starts to melt, bubble and crisp up.
5. Dive into the cheesy crust and serve in bowls. Enjoy as is, or with long-grain rice, avocado and cilantro.

PREP TIME: **10 MINUTES**
COOK TIME: **2 HOURS**
DIFFICULTY: **EASY**
SERVES: **4**
MEAT

SHEET-PAN TANDOORI SUNDAY ROAST

Top your roast chicken and veggies with that flames tandoori twist! All in one pan for EASE. You're welcome. Careful here that your chicken is cooked: give it 15-20 minutes per pound (455 g) and work out how long yours needs by weighing it before you cook it.

INGREDIENTS

For the quick curry paste

1 tablespoon garam masala
1 tablespoon chili powder
1 teaspoon salt
2 tablespoons garlic paste
2 tablespoons unsalted butter, at room temperature
6 tablespoons olive oil

For the chicken and vegetables

1 large organic chicken (roughly 4 pounds [1.8 kg])
2 pounds (910 g) new potatoes
3 large carrots, cut into chunky batons
1 head of broccoli, cut into large florets
2 cups (480 ml) chicken stock

All in one pan for EASE. You're welcome.

METHOD

1. Preheat the oven to 400°F (200°C, or gas mark 6). In a small bowl, combine the curry paste ingredients until smooth. Weigh your chicken and calculate its cooking time (see recipe introduction).
2. Place a wire rack over a large, deep roasting pan and lay the chicken on top. Smooth half of the curry paste over the chicken, ensuring it is evenly coated. Cover the chicken with foil and transfer to the oven.
3. Put the vegetables into a large bowl and spoon over the remaining curry paste. Massage the vegetables with your hands, ensuring they are well coated. Cover and set aside.
4. After 50 minutes, remove the chicken from the oven. Remove the foil, carefully lift the wire rack off the roasting pan and set the chicken aside. Pour any juices from the roasting pan into a small bowl or mug. Lay the vegetables across the bottom of the roasting pan and rest the wire rack with the chicken back on top.
5. Pour the juices over the chicken to baste it, then return to the oven for 35 minutes, or as long as your calculation told you, until the vegetables and chicken are cooked through and the chicken skin is golden and crisp. If the chicken skin starts to brown too much at any point, cover it with foil.
6. Remove the chicken and vegetables from the oven. Insert a skewer into the thickest part of the chicken breast to check if it is cooked through; the skewer should come out piping hot and the juices from the meat should run clear. Transfer the chicken to a board to rest for at least 15 minutes and spoon the vegetables into a heated serving dish, leaving any juices in the pan. Cover the chicken and vegetarians with foil to keep in the heat.
7. Place the roasting pan on the stove top over medium–low heat. Once the juices start to bubble, pour in a large splash of stock. Bring to a simmer and, using a wooden spoon, scrape the pan to loosen any residue. Pour in the rest of the stock and increase the heat a little. Allow the gravy to simmer and reduce for 15 minutes.
8. Carve the chicken and serve up with the vegetarians and a generous ladle of tandoori–infused gravy. Dig in!

DIY CHICKEN SHAWARMA KEBABS

PREP TIME: **10 MINUTES + MARINATING**

COOK TIME: **1 HOUR**

DIFFICULTY: **EASY**

SERVES: **4**

MEAT

Be your own boss and whip up our mouthwatering chicken shawarma kebabs. Go all out with juicy marinated chicken, flatbread, VEGETARIANs... the full works.

INGREDIENTS

For the marinade

⅔ cup (160 g) plain yogurt

2 teaspoons chili powder

2 teaspoons garam masala

1 teaspoon salt

1 tablespoon garlic paste

1 tablespoon Dijon mustard

juice of ½ lemon

For the kebabs

8 skinless, boneless chicken thighs

1 large onion, peeled

8 flatbread wraps

mixed salad (cucumbers, tomatoes, carrot, red cabbage, lettuce)

4 tablespoons harissa mayonnaise

METHOD

1. In a large bowl, combine the marinade ingredients and add the chicken thighs, ensuring they are well coated. Cover and place in the refrigerator for at least 30 minutes, or overnight, to marinate.
2. Remove from the refrigerator and allow to come to room temperature. Meanwhile, soak 3 wooden skewers in a bowl of water.
3. Preheat the oven to 350°F (180°C, or gas mark 4).
4. Slice the onion in half and place one half, flat-side down, in the center of a baking sheet. Push 2 skewers vertically into the onion, one on the left and one on the right. Slide the chicken thighs down the skewers so both skewers pierce each thigh, layering them up, one on top of the other. Carefully slide a third skewer down through the middle of the chicken and onion for added support, making sure it, too, pierces each thigh. Top with the second onion half, flat-side down, to hold the skewers in place.
5. Transfer to the oven (ensure there is enough space for the construction to stand upright) and cook for 1 hour until the chicken is cooked through, compact and golden with caramelized edges.
6. Remove from the oven and allow to rest for 10 minutes before serving.
7. Slice the chicken vertically and serve in flatbreads, over a bed of mixed salad. Finish with a generous drizzle of harissa mayonnaise and enjoy!

CHILI BEEF MOODLES

PREP TIME: **10 MINUTES**
COOK TIME: **15 MINUTES**
DIFFICULTY: **EASY**
SERVES: **4**
MEAT

Imagine a bowl full of noodz with crispy caramelized ground beef, fresh veggies, a chili oil kick, a little sweet honey and salty soy. OOOOOFT.

INGREDIENTS

1 tablespoon vegetable oil

4 scallions, sliced

2 garlic cloves, very finely chopped

4 red chilies, sliced (seeds in or out, depending on spice preference)

1 pound (455 g) ground beef

2 carrots, sliced into fine matchsticks

2 heads bok choy, sliced

4 tablespoons soy sauce

3 tablespoons honey

2 tablespoons hot chili sauce

8 ounces (224 g) cooked flat rice noodles

sesame seeds and cilantro, to serve (optional)

METHOD

1. Heat the vegetable oil in a large frying pan over medium heat and soften the scallions, garlic and chilies. Increase the heat to high and add the beef, breaking it up with a wooden spoon as it cooks. Fry for 10 minutes, or until browned.
2. Add the carrots, bok choy, soy sauce, honey and chili sauce. Stir-fry for a further 5 minutes, until the vegetables are al dente and the beef is crispy and starting to caramelize in the sauce.
3. Remove from the heat and toss with the flat rice noodles, ensuring they are well coated in the sauce and crispy beef.
4. Divide the noodles among 4 warmed bowls and serve, topped with sesame seeds and cilantro, if you like.

CAUGHT FAKIN'

CAUGHT QUIZ

WHICH CAUGHT CHEF ARE YOU?

Listen, if you have this cookbook, you're in the gang, but obviously we have to see what sort of chefileeni you are. Take this quiz and find out.

You like cooking for the gang?

Yes, my G.

I always have the mandem over.

You best know my food is for ME.

Have you got people asking you for chefileeni wisdom?

I'm a guru, fam.

Keeping my hacks to myself.

Do people vibe with you while you chef it up?

I'm cheffing up good vibes only.

The only thing I'm vibing with is my food.

How full is your fridge?

My shelves are STACKED.

I'm hitting up the store every time.

Gang every time.

BOUGIE CHEF

IS THAT YOU, YEAH? Sorry, we don't cook with golden spatulas like you, fam. Get yourself a palace and swim in gold.

CHILL CHEF

If you're chill, then you are defo a part of the Caught Snackin' GANG! Come through to the TikTok HQ and grab an apron, I'm tired.

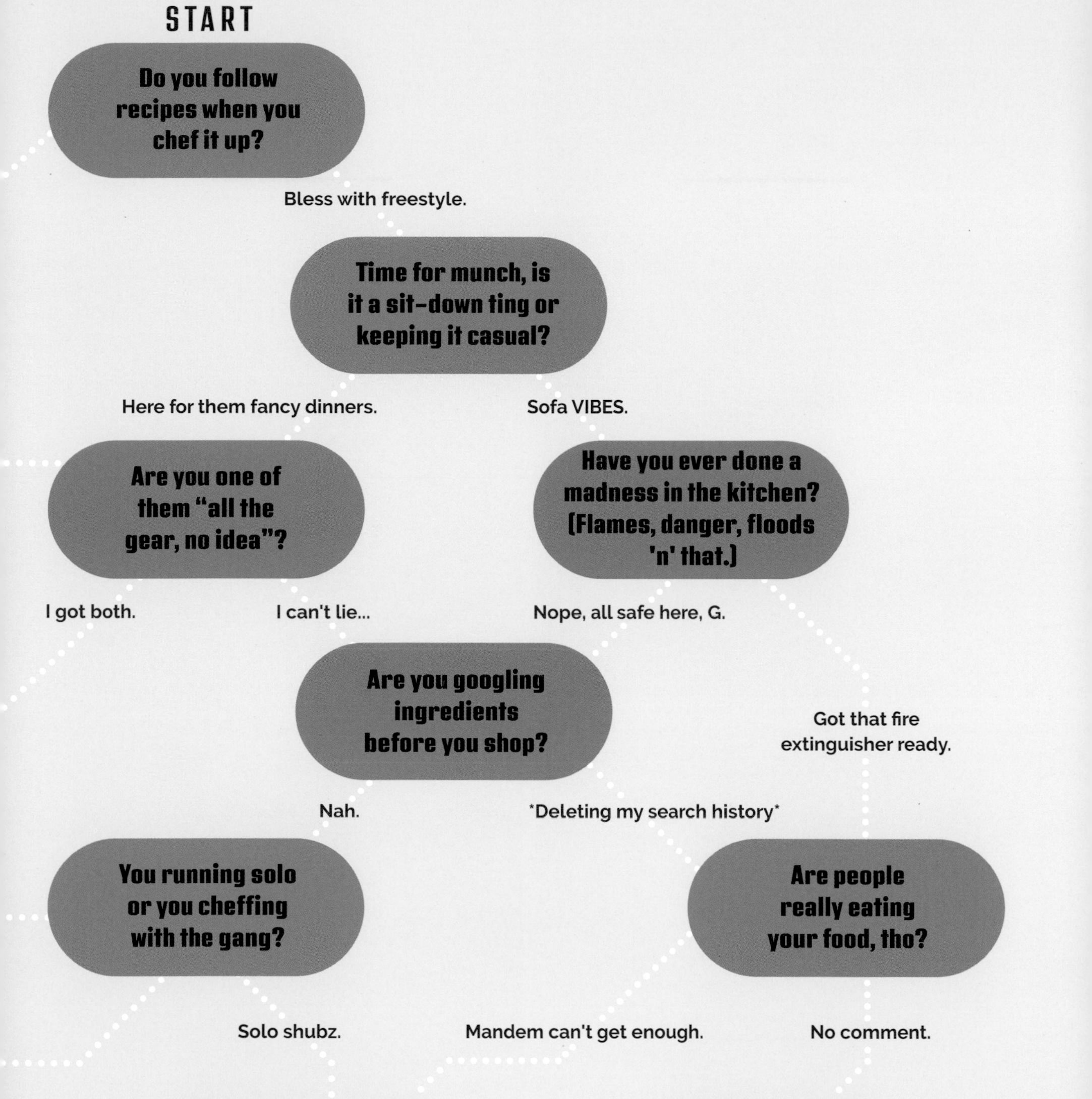

START

Do you follow recipes when you chef it up?

Bless with freestyle.

Time for munch, is it a sit-down ting or keeping it casual?

Here for them fancy dinners.

Sofa VIBES.

Are you one of them "all the gear, no idea"?

Have you ever done a madness in the kitchen? (Flames, danger, floods 'n' that.)

I got both.

I can't lie...

Nope, all safe here, G.

Are you googling ingredients before you shop?

Got that fire extinguisher ready.

Nah.

Deleting my search history

You running solo or you cheffing with the gang?

Are people really eating your food, tho?

Solo shubz.

Mandem can't get enough.

No comment.

STRESS CHEF

I appreciate you stressin' just means you care, but don't come at me with your bad vibes and energies, chef.

DEAD CHEF

If you've reached this point, you may as well go to bed. You can't handle it. Just drink water, innit. It's a takeaway ting for you, G.

A molten mozzarella middle for the mandem

CHEESY GARLIC-BUTTER DOUGH BALLS

PREP TIME: **10 MINUTES**
COOK TIME: **25 MINUTES**
DIFFICULTY: **EASY**
SERVES: **2 (as a snack or starter, makes around 10)**
VEGETARIAN

These DECADENT garlic-"bootah" balls are stuffed with a molten mozzarella middle for the mandem.

INGREDIENTS

6 tablespoons (90 g) salted butter, at room temperature

2 tablespoons finely chopped parsley leaves

3 garlic cloves, very finely chopped

1½ cups (180 g) self-rising flour, plus more to dust

1 teaspoon salt

¾ cup (180 g) Greek-style yogurt

10 mozzarella cheese pearls, drained and patted dry with paper towels

METHOD

1. Preheat the oven to 350°F (180°C, or gas mark 4). Line a baking sheet with parchment paper.
2. In a medium-sized bowl, combine the butter, parsley and garlic. Put half the garlic butter mix in a small saucepan and gently melt over low heat.
3. Sift the flour into a large bowl and add the salt and yogurt. Roughly bring the ingredients together with a wooden spoon or spatula, then go in with your hands and shape the mixture into a ball. Transfer to a lightly floured surface. Knead for a couple of minutes until you have a smooth, firm dough.
4. Divide the dough into 10 balls. Flatten the balls and place a mozzarella pearl in the center of each one, then shape the dough around the mozzarella, pressing the edges together to seal. Place the dough balls on the prepared baking sheet and brush with the melted garlic butter.
5. Bake for 20 minutes, or until golden and melting in the middle.
6. Serve with the remaining garlic butter, melted, for dipping.

VEGGIE KATSU CURRY

PREP TIME: **15 MINUTES**
COOK TIME: **45 MINUTES**
DIFFICULTY: **EASY**
SERVES: **2**
VEGETARIAN

Katsu curry will always be a personal fave and this veggie version is no joke! Douse golden slices of panko-coated eggplant in creamy katsu sauce and don't look back.

INGREDIENTS

1 cup (120 g) panko breadcrumbs
⅔ cup (80 g) all-purpose flour
2 eggs, lightly beaten
salt and pepper
1 large eggplant, sliced into thick rounds
1 recipe katsu curry sauce (see page 157)
1 cup (250 g) cooked jasmine rice, to serve

To serve (optional)

cilantro leaves
sesame seeds
fresh garden salad

METHOD

1. Preheat the oven to 400°F (200°C, or gas mark 6).
2. Pour the panko breadcrumbs onto a baking sheet and toast in the oven for 8–10 minutes until pale golden. Remove from the oven and allow to cool for 10 minutes or so. Leave the oven on.
3. Put the flour, eggs and toasted panko crumbs into 3 separate bowls. Generously season the flour with salt and pepper, then turn the eggplant slices in it, ensuring they are evenly coated. Tap off any excess flour, then dip the eggplant slices in the egg, followed by the toasted crumbs.
4. Lay the coated eggplant slices on a wire rack set over a baking sheet and bake for 30–35 minutes until golden and crisp with soft centers.
5. Meanwhile, make the katsu sauce.
6. Remove the eggplant slices from the oven and serve with jasmine rice, with the katsu sauce generously spooned over. Scatter with cilantro and sesame seeds, and eat with a fresh garden salad, if you like.

PREP TIME: **10 MINUTES**
COOK TIME: **35 MINUTES**
DIFFICULTY: **EASY**
SERVES: **2**
MEAT

PERI PERI CHICKEN BURGER

Thought you knew where to get your favorite peri peri chicken? THINK AGAIN. Make your own at home and turn the flames dial UP.

INGREDIENTS

For the peri peri sauce

1 red pepper, roughly chopped
1 red chile, deseeded
1 garlic clove
2 teaspoons smoked paprika
2 tablespoons olive oil

For the burgers

2 skinless, boneless chicken thighs
2 tablespoons mayonnaise
2 soft white burger buns
2 Cheddar cheese slices
4 large lettuce leaves
¼ cup (60 g) store-bought coleslaw
1 large tomato, sliced (optional)
½ red onion, sliced (optional)

METHOD

1. Preheat the oven to 400°F (200°C, or gas mark 6).
2. Start with the sauce. Put the red pepper, chile, garlic, paprika and olive oil in a blender and purée to form a smooth sauce.
3. Lay the chicken thighs flat in a shallow bowl or dish. Pour three-quarters of the sauce over them, ensuring they are well coated. Combine the remaining sauce with the mayonnaise to make a peri peri mayo.
4. Toast the buns in a frying pan over medium-high heat for 2–3 minutes.
5. Fry the chicken thighs in the same pan over high heat for 5 minutes on each side until charred. Transfer them to the oven and cook for a further 20 minutes. In the final 5 minutes of cooking time, top each thigh with a slice of Cheddar cheese and allow to melt.
6. Spread the buns with peri peri mayo, then fill with lettuce, coleslaw, tomato and onion slices (if you like), along with the juicy, cheesy chicken thighs.

GIN & TONIC FISH & CHIPS

PREP TIME: **15 MINUTES + CHILLING**
COOK TIME: **30 MINUTES**
DIFFICULTY: **ADVANCED**
SERVES: **2**
FISH

These bougie, boozy battered fillets will have you craving fish Friday! Finessed with crispy, chunky chips and green peas OBVS.

INGREDIENTS

For the batter

¾ cup (90 g) all-purpose flour, plus more to lightly coat the fish

½ teaspoon salt

⅔ cup (160 ml) tonic water

2 tablespoons (30 ml) gin

For the fish and chips

10 ounces (300 g) frozen thick-cut french fries

2 cups (480 ml) vegetable oil

2 haddock or cod fillets, about 5 ounces (140 g) each

To serve

tartar sauce

lemon wedges

cooked green peas

TIP:
The bubbles in the tonic water make for an extra crunchy, light batter. No tonic water? Use sparkling water instead.

METHOD

1. Preheat the oven to 425°F (220°C, or gas mark 7).
2. Put the flour and salt into a medium-sized bowl and gradually pour in the tonic water, stirring until you have a smooth batter. Add the gin and stir to combine. Cover and chill in the refrigerator for at least 20 minutes.
3. Arrange the french fries on a large baking sheet and bake for 15–20 minutes, or according to the package instructions.
4. Pour the vegetable oil into a large, deep saucepan with a well-fitting lid and set over medium heat until it reaches 350°F (180°C). (See page 17 for deep-frying hacks.)
5. When the batter has sufficiently chilled, remove from the refrigerator. Pat dry the fish fillets with paper towels and turn them in all-purpose flour to lightly coat, then dip them in the batter, ensuring they are evenly coated.
6. When the oil has reached 350°F (180°C), carefully add the battered fillets and fry for 5-7 minutes, until golden, crisp and cooked through. Remove the fillets from the oil and place on a plate double-lined with paper towels to drain off any excess oil.
7. Serve the battered fish with the chunky chips, tartar sauce, lemon wedges and peas.

MIGHTY MEATBALL SUB

PREP TIME: **15 MINUTES**
COOK TIME: **30 MINUTES**
DIFFICULTY: **EASY**
SERVES: **2**
MEAT

Our big boi meatball sub will fill the heart, soul and stomach for DAYS.

INGREDIENTS

For the meatballs

1 tablespoon olive oil

¼ onion, grated

2 garlic cloves, very finely chopped

¼ pound (115 g) ground beef

¼ pound (115 g) ground pork

1 teaspoon Italian mixed dried herbs

1 tablespoon finely grated Parmesan cheese

1 egg, lightly beaten

salt and pepper

For the sub

1 (8-ounce [224-g]) jar tomato and basil sauce

¼ teaspoon red pepper flakes

2 small baguettes or sub rolls

6 mozzarella cheese slices

2 basil sprigs

METHOD

1. Preheat the oven to 375ºF (190ºC, or gas mark 5).
2. Heat the olive oil in a large frying pan over low heat and sweat the onion and garlic for 5 minutes until softened.
3. Transfer to a medium-sized bowl and combine with the beef, pork, dried herbs, Parmesan and egg, and season with salt and pepper.
4. Divide the mixture into 10 balls and place on a baking sheet. Bake for 15 minutes until golden and cooked through. After 15 minutes, remove the meatballs from the oven and preheat the broiler to medium.
5. Meanwhile, pour the tomato and basil sauce into the frying pan you used for the onions and bring to a gentle simmer over medium-low heat. Add the baked meatballs and sprinkle with the red pepper flakes, then cover and simmer for 10-15 minutes until the sauce has thickened.
6. Cut the baguettes or subs in half lengthwise. Divide the meatballs between them and spoon over the tomato sauce. Top with the mozzarella slices and basil and place under the broiler for 3-5 minutes, until the cheese is melted and bubbling. Enjoy immediately.

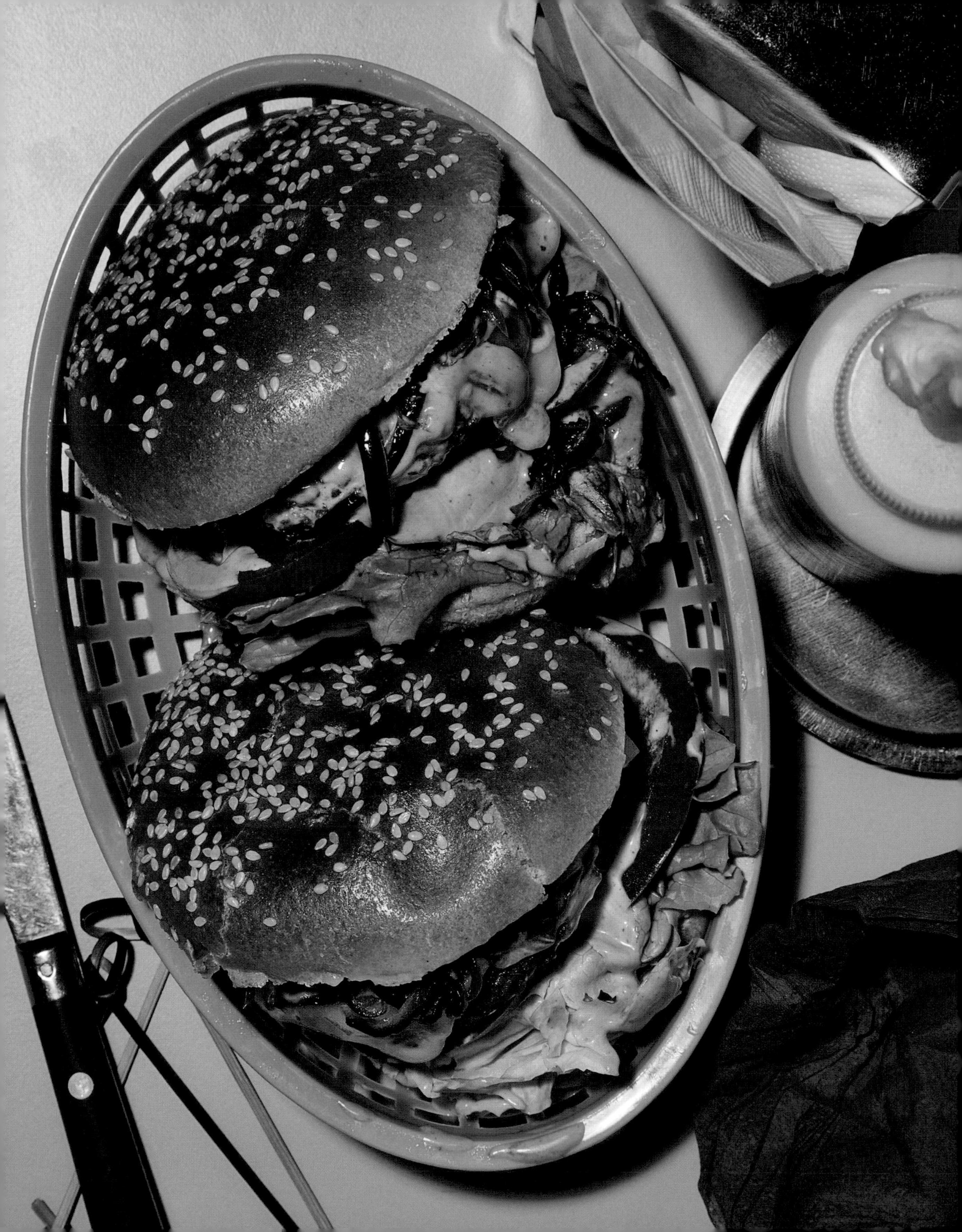

PLANT BURGER WITH SECRET SAUCE

PREP TIME: **10 MINUTES**
COOK TIME: **20 MINUTES**
DIFFICULTY: **EASY**
SERVES: **2**
VEGAN

LISTEN, don't say we don't spoil you guys when we're out here dishing out our Caught SECRET sauce that slaps with this plant burger. Keep this between us, yeah? Safe.

INGREDIENTS

For the burger sauce

2 tablespoons vegan mayonnaise
1 tablespoon tomato ketchup
1 tablespoon sriracha
1 tablespoon mustard
1 tablespoon finely chopped pickle (optional)
salt and pepper

For the burgers

1 tablespoon olive oil
½ red onion, sliced into rounds
2 vegan burgers
2 vegan burger cheese slices
2 brioche burger buns, halved
1 head curly leaf lettuce
1 large tomato, sliced

METHOD

1. In a small bowl, combine the burger sauce ingredients. Taste and season accordingly with salt and pepper.
2. Heat the oil in a frying pan over a low-medium heat and sweat the onion for 10 minutes or so, until soft and caramelized. Transfer to a small bowl.
3. In the same pan, fry the burgers according to the package instructions. In the final minute of cooking, add a slice of cheese to the top of each one. Set the burgers aside while you toast the buns in the same frying pan.
4. Generously spread the toasted buns with burger sauce and layer up with curly lettuce leaves, tomato slices, a burger with melted cheese and the sweet caramelized onions. Top with a burger-bun lid and enjoy immediately.

PREP TIME: **10 MINUTES**
COOK TIME: **1 HOUR**
DIFFICULTY: **ADVANCED**
SERVES: **6–8**
MEAT

FRIED CHICKEN BUCKET

When the mandem roll through, best know this crispy, succulent fried chicken bucket will have them feeling satisfied. You will make a lot of friends with this bucket... you heard it here first.

INGREDIENTS

For the seasoned flour

5 cups (600 g) all-purpose flour
4 teaspoons Italian mixed dried herbs
4 teaspoons chili powder
4 teaspoons hot paprika
4 teaspoons garlic powder
4 teaspoons onion powder
2 teaspoons pepper
4 teaspoons salt

For the fried chicken

4 eggs, lightly beaten
2½ cups (600 ml) buttermilk
4 cups (960 ml) vegetable or sunflower oil, to deep-fry
2¼ pounds (1 kg) skinless, boneless chicken thighs
2¼ pounds (1 kg) skinless, boneless chicken drumsticks

To serve (optional)

grilled corn cobettes
baked beans
french fries

METHOD

1. Combine the seasoned flour ingredients in a medium-sized bowl.
2. Whisk the egg and buttermilk in a separate bowl.
3. Pour the oil into a large, deep saucepan with a well-fitting lid and set over medium heat. (See page 17 for deep-frying hacks.) Preheat the oven to 250°F (120°C, or gas mark ½).
4. Pat dry all of the chicken thighs and drumsticks with paper towels. Dip them in the egg mixture and then the seasoned flour. Repeat to double-coat the chicken, for extra crunch!
5. When the oil has reached 350°F (180°C), cook the coated chicken in batches for 15 minutes, until golden, super crisp and cooked through. Drain off any excess oil on a plate double-lined with paper towels. Spread out the cooked chicken on a baking sheet and keep warm in the oven while you cook the rest.
6. Serve the chicken pieces, piled high, with corn, beans and french fries on the side.

MEATLESS BEAN & CHEEZ MELTS

PREP TIME: **15 MINUTES**
COOK TIME: **40 MINUTES**
DIFFICULTY: **EASY**
SERVES: **4**
VEGAN

This baked goodie is a sensational crowd-pleaser: hot puff-pastry pockets of melted cheese, baked beans and vegan sausage.

INGREDIENTS

4 vegan sausages

1 (17-ounce [500-g]) package vegan puff pastry

2 tablespoons all-purpose flour, to dust

8 tablespoons baked beans

¾ cup (75 g) grated vegan Cheddar-style cheese

6 tablespoons (90 g) vegan, non-dairy spread, melted

METHOD

1. Preheat the oven to 375°F (190°C, or gas mark 5) and line a baking sheet with parchment paper.
2. Lay the sausages on a baking sheet and cook in the oven for 15 minutes, or according to the package instructions. Allow them to cool, then cut in half lengthwise. Leave the oven on.
3. Roll out the pastry on a lightly floured surface and cut it into 4 even rectangles. Position one of the pieces of pastry with a long side facing you and top the right-hand side with 2 tablespoons of baked beans, 2 sausage halves and a handful of grated cheese, leaving a border around the edge.
4. Brush the borders of the pastry with the melted spread.
5. Fold the left side of the pastry over the filling so the edges meet. Crimp with a fork to seal the pastry and score the top with a sharp knife. Repeat to make the other 3 parcels.
6. Arrange the pastries on the prepared baking sheet. Brush with more melted spread and then bake for 25 minutes until golden and puffed up. Allow to cool for 5 minutes before serving.

GLAZED VANILLA DOUGHNUTS

PREP TIME: **10 MINUTES + CHILLING**
COOK TIME: **12 MINUTES**
DIFFICULTY: **EASY**
SERVES: **2**
VEGETARIAN

When Homer Simpson said, "Mmmmmmm.... doughnuts," you best believe he was referencing these.

INGREDIENTS

1¼ cups (160 g) self-rising flour
6 tablespoons (75 g) caster sugar
¾ cup (180 g) full-fat yogurt, or more as needed
2 cups (480 ml) vegetable or sunflower oil
2 cups (240 g) powdered sugar
5 tablespoons (75 ml) milk
1 teaspoon vanilla extract
rainbow sprinkles (optional)

METHOD

1. In a medium-sized bowl, combine the flour, caster sugar and yogurt until you have a smooth, thick mixture. Cover and chill in the refrigerator for 15 minutes.
2. Heat the oil, in a large, deep saucepan with a well-fitting lid, to 350°F (180°C). (See page 17 for deep-frying hacks.)
3. Use an ice-cream scoop to carefully scoop portions of the chilled batter into the hot oil. Fry in batches for 5-6 minutes, until golden and cooked through with a dense yet fluffy center. These doughnuts have a delicious cakey texture!
4. Remove the doughnuts from the oil and drain off the excess oil on a plate double-lined with paper towels.
5. Meanwhile, make the glaze by combining the powdered sugar, milk and vanilla extract in a shallow bowl.
6. Roll the doughnuts in the glaze and lay them out across a wire rack for about 15 minutes, or until the glaze has set. Enjoy as they are, or top with rainbow sprinkles to serve.

TIP:
Skewer a hole in the doughnuts and squeeze in chocolate sauce to level up.

PREP TIME: **5 MINUTES**
COOK TIME: **NONE**
DIFFICULTY: **EASY**
SERVES: **2**
VEGETARIAN

FAKE IT ICED MOCHA

Who wants to line up to have some mediocre coffee? With this tasty caffeinated bevi, you'll become a barista in your own kitchen! Light work.

INGREDIENTS

2 large handfuls ice cubes

2 shots freshly brewed espresso

1 cup (240 ml) chilled milk (dairy or plant-based)

1 tablespoon chocolate syrup, plus more to serve

1 teaspoon sugar

whipped cream, to serve

METHOD

1. Wrap half of the ice cubes in a clean tea towel and bash with a rolling pin to crush into small pieces.
2. Put the crushed ice into a blender with the espresso, milk, chocolate syrup and sugar. Blend for 30 seconds, until well combined.
3. Pour into tall glasses over the remaining ice cubes. Top with whipped cream and a drizzle of chocolate syrup and get slurpin'.

CAUGHT BAKIN'

2- OR 3-INGREDIENT BAKES

You know them lazy days, but you're craving them SWEET ONES? These simple bakes will have your back.

2-INGREDIENT

CHOCOLATE COOKIES

PREP TIME: **2 MINUTES**

COOK TIME: **10 MINUTES**

DIFFICULTY: **EASY**

MAKES: **10–12**

VEGETARIAN

INGREDIENTS

¾ cup plus 1 tablespoon (200 g) chocolate hazelnut spread, such as Nutella

⅔ cup (80 g) all-purpose flour

METHOD

1. Preheat the oven to 350°F (180°C, or gas mark 4). Line a baking sheet with parchment paper.
2. Combine the Nutella and flour in a large bowl until you have a thick, smooth mixture.
3. Divide and roll the mixture into even-sized balls and place on the prepared baking sheet.
4. Gently squash each ball a little with a teaspoon and bake the cookies for 10 minutes, until cooked through with a cakey consistency.
5. Allow to cool a little before serving.

2-INGREDIENT

CHOCOLATE SOUFFLÉ

PREP TIME: **10 MINUTES**

COOK TIME: **15–20 MINUTES**

DIFFICULTY: **EASY**

SERVES: **2**

VEGETARIAN

INGREDIENTS

2 eggs, separated

⅔ cup (160 g) chocolate hazelnut spread, such as Nutella

METHOD

1. Preheat the oven to 375°F (190°C, or gas mark 5).
2. Whisk the egg yolks in a medium-sized bowl. Add the Nutella and stir until you have a smooth paste.
3. Whisk the egg whites in another medium-sized bowl for about 2 minutes until they form stiff peaks.
4. Fold the egg whites into the Nutella mixture. Pour into 2 ramekins, leaving about ½ inch (1 cm) at the top.
5. Bake for 15-20 minutes until puffed up and cooked on the outside with a soft, melting center. Do not open the oven door while baking, or the soufflé won't rise. Serve immediately.

2-INGREDIENT

CHOCOLATE MOUSSE

PREP TIME: **10 MINUTES**

COOK TIME: **NONE**

DIFFICULTY: **EASY**

SERVES: **2**

VEGAN

INGREDIENTS

7 ounces (200 g) dark chocolate

⅔ cup (160 ml) just-boiled water

1 cup (240 g) ice cubes

METHOD

1. Break the chocolate into small pieces, place in a medium heatproof bowl and pour in the water. Stir until the chocolate has completely melted into the water.
2. Set the bowl over another larger bowl containing the ice cubes and whisk the chocolate mixture, using an electric mixer, for 2-3 minutes, until thick and fluffy.
3. Spoon into 2 individual glasses and serve immediately, or keep in the refrigerator for later. These will keep in the refrigerator for up to 3 days.

3-INGREDIENT

CRÈME BRÛLÉE

PREP TIME: **5 MINUTES + CHILLING**

COOK TIME: **30 MINUTES**

DIFFICULTY: **EASY**

SERVES: **4**

VEGETARIAN

INGREDIENTS

2 cups (480 g) tub of vanilla ice cream, melted

4 egg yolks

4 tablespoons sugar

METHOD

1. Place a deep baking dish in the oven. Preheat the oven to 325°F (170°C, or gas mark 3). Bring a kettle of water to a boil.
2. Whisk together the melted ice cream and egg yolks until combined and pour this into 4 ovenproof ramekins.
3. Place the ramekins in the heated baking dish. Pour in just-boiled water from the kettle so that it comes three-quarters of the way up the sides of the ramekins.
4. Bake for 25–30 minutes, then remove the ramekins from the baking dish. The crème should have a firm jiggle to it when tapped. Cover the ramekins and place them in the refrigerator to cool.
5. Once cool, sprinkle over a layer of sugar. Preheat the broiler to medium and broil until the sugar has melted to a deep golden brown. Allow the sugar to cool, then place in the refrigerator for 30 minutes to set, or until you are ready to serve. These will keep in the refrigerator for up to 3 days.

These simple bakes will have your back

3-INGREDIENT

CHOCOLATE ICE CREAM CAKE

PREP TIME: **5 MINUTES**

COOK TIME: **35–40 MINUTES**

DIFFICULTY: **EASY**

SERVES: **8**

VEGETARIAN

INGREDIENTS

2 cups (480 g) tub of chocolate ice cream, melted

1½ cups (180 g) self-rising flour

1 cup (170 g) milk chocolate chips

METHOD

1. Preheat the oven to 350°F (180°C, or gas mark 4). Line a loaf pan with parchment paper.
2. Mix the melted ice cream and flour in a large bowl until smooth and well combined.
3. Fold in the chocolate chips and pour the mixture into the prepared pan.
4. Bake for 35-40 minutes, or until a skewer inserted into the middle comes out clean.
5. Allow to cool in the pan, then turn out and slice to serve.

3-INGREDIENT

VANILLA CUPCAKES

PREP TIME: **5 MINUTES**

COOK TIME: **20–25 MINUTES**

DIFFICULTY: **EASY**

MAKES: **6–8**

VEGETARIAN

INGREDIENTS

1 (9-ounce [250-g]) package vanilla cake mix

1 cup (240 g) full-fat mayonnaise

1 (14-ounce [400-g]) can vanilla frosting

METHOD

1. Preheat the oven to 350°F (180°C, or gas mark 4). Line a muffin pan with 6-8 cupcake liners.
2. Combine the cake mix and mayonnaise in a large bowl until smooth.
3. Distribute the cake mixture evenly among the prepared cupcake liners.
4. Bake for 20-25 minutes, or until cooked through, then remove the cupcakes from the pan and allow to cool on a wire rack. Top with frosting and enjoy.

PREP TIME: **5 MINUTES**
COOK TIME: **75 SECONDS**
DIFFICULTY: **EASY**
MAKES: **1**
VEGETARIAN

CHOCOLATE MUG CAKE

Don't be a mug; try this cake.

INGREDIENTS

2 tablespoons (28 g) salted butter, at room temperature
¼ cup (50 g) caster sugar
3 tablespoons boiling water
2 tablespoons cocoa powder
¼ cup (30 g) self-rising flour
¼ teaspoon salt
1 tablespoon chocolate chips

METHOD

1. Put the butter, caster sugar and boiling water in a microwaveable mug and stir until melted.
2. Add the cocoa powder, flour and salt and stir until well combined and smooth.
3. Fold in the chocolate chips and microwave on high for 1 minute 15 seconds, or until baked on top with a soft, gooey center. Dig in with a spoon!

TIP:
Prep these in advance and refrigerate. Just toss them in the microwave when ready to serve.

GIANT PAN COOKIE

PREP TIME: **10 MINUTES**
COOK TIME: **12 MINUTES**
DIFFICULTY: **EASY**
SERVES: **4**
VEGETARIAN

Gooey cookies are good and that. But one in GIANT form? Oozing all over the place, on my plate, on your plate? It's great, just make it.

INGREDIENTS

½ cup (120 g) unsalted butter, plus more for the pan

¼ cup (50 g) light brown sugar

¼ cup (50 g) caster sugar

1 egg, plus 1 egg yolk

1 teaspoon vanilla extract

1⅓ cups (160 g) all-purpose flour

½ teaspoon baking soda

generous pinch of salt

3½ ounces (100 g) milk or dark chocolate, roughly chopped

vanilla ice cream, to serve (optional)

METHOD

1. Preheat the oven to 350°F (180°C, or gas mark 4).
2. In a large bowl, combine the butter and both sugars until you have a smooth, thick paste. Add the egg, egg yolk and vanilla and mix until smooth.
3. Sift in the flour, baking soda and salt, and mix once more. You should have a thick, sticky dough.
4. Fold in the chopped chocolate and form the dough into a large ball.
5. Butter an ovenproof frying pan or skillet and add the cookie dough. Flatten the dough with your hands and press it out to fill the base of the pan.
6. Transfer to the oven and bake for 12 minutes until the cookie is golden but still soft and gooey in the center, with melting chocolate pieces.
7. Present the cookie in the pan with 4 large scoops of ice cream in the center. Spoon the cookie and melting ice cream into bowls to serve. Alternatively, dive straight in with spoons for the ultimate sharer!

STRAWBERRIES & CREAM FUDGE

PREP TIME: **10 MINUTES + CHILLING**
COOK TIME: **5 MINUTES**
DIFFICULTY: **EASY**
SERVES: **10**
VEGETARIAN

If you're blessed with a sweet tooth, whip up this NAWTY pink white-choc-and-strawberry fudge in 15 minutes.

INGREDIENTS

knob of butter, for the pan
14 ounces (400 g) white chocolate
1 (14-ounce [400-g]) can condensed milk
3 tablespoons strawberry milkshake powder
1 teaspoon pink food coloring
7 ounces (200 g) strawberries-and-cream chocolate truffles

METHOD

1. Butter a loaf pan and line the bottom and sides with parchment paper.
2. Melt the white chocolate in a heatproof bowl set over a saucepan of *very* gently simmering water, making sure the bowl doesn't touch the water. This should take about 5 minutes. (White chocolate has a high percentage of milk fats, giving it a lower melting point than milk and dark chocolate, so melting it over very gentle heat means it won't burn and seize up.)
3. Meanwhile, whisk together the condensed milk, strawberry milkshake powder and pink food coloring in a small bowl.
4. Once the white chocolate has fully melted, stir in the condensed milk mixture until fully combined. Stir half of the truffles into the fudge mix, then pour it into the prepared pan.
5. Roughly chop the remaining truffles and sprinkle them on. Place in the refrigerator for at least 4 hours, or until firm.
6. Once set, turn out and slice into slabs to serve.

TIP:
Swap strawberry milkshake powder for chocolate flavor and swap the truffles for chocolates.

PREP TIME: **20 MINUTES + CHILLING**

COOK TIME: **NONE**

DIFFICULTY: **EASY**

SERVES: **8–10**

VEGETARIAN

PARTY BISCUIT CHEESECAKE

Bring this to the next shubz for all the sweet vibes. LET'S GO.

INGREDIENTS

10 tablespoons (150 g) melted unsalted butter, plus more for the pan

1 pound (455 g) iced round cookies

3 (8-ounce [224-g]) packages full-fat cream cheese

1¼ cups (300 ml) heavy cream

¾ cup (90 g) powdered sugar

1 teaspoon vanilla extract

METHOD

1. Butter an 8-inch (20-cm) springform cake pan.
2. Put half the biscuits into a medium-sized bowl. Use a rolling pin to crush them into fine crumbs. Pour in the melted butter, mix and transfer to the prepared pan. Use the back of a spoon to press the crumb mixture tightly into the base of the cake pan. Put in the refrigerator to chill while you make the filling.
3. Put the cream cheese, heavy cream, powdered sugar and vanilla extract into a large mixing bowl and whip for 2-3 minutes until thick and silky. Be careful not to overwhip, or the mixture will turn cakey in texture.
4. Remove the cake pan from the refrigerator. Spoon the cream filling over the crumb base, top with the remaining cookies and return to the refrigerator for at least 1 hour, until set.
5. Unlatch the springform pan and remove. Place the cheesecake on a board or plate and slice to serve.

SKY-HIGH BANAYNAY SUNDAE

PREP TIME: **5 MINUTES + FREEZING**

COOK TIME: **NONE**

DIFFICULTY: **EASY**

SERVES: **2**

VEGETARIAN

GET HIGH on sugar with this banging banaynay sundae. Literal flavors, towered with cookies, cream, caramel sauce and our very own honeycomb (little recipe inception ting).

INGREDIENTS

6 large bananas

2 tablespoons honeycomb (for Caught's DIY Honeycomb, see pages 48–9), crumbled

6 speculoos cookies, such as Lotus, roughly crushed

whipped cream

½ cup (120 ml) store-bought salted caramel sauce

2 ounces (60 g) milk chocolate, roughly chopped

METHOD

1. Peel and slice the bananas and spread them out on a plate or tray. Cover with plastic wrap and freeze for at least 3 hours. (Now would be a good time to make our DIY Honeycomb, if you are going to make your own.)
2. Once out of the freezer, put the chopped bananas into a food processor or high-powered blender and pulse to break up the slices. Scrape down the sides of the blender and continue to pulse until the banana thickens to a smooth, sticky, creamy paste.
3. Spoon the banana paste into an airtight container and freeze for another hour, or serve immediately if you like it on the softer side.
4. When ready to serve, scoop the banana ice cream into 2 tall glasses, crumbling the cookies over the top as you go. Adorn with whipped cream, salted caramel sauce, a handful of chopped chocolate and the crumbled honeycomb. Dig in!

PREP TIME: **10 MINUTES**
COOK TIME: **12 MINUTES**
DIFFICULTY: **EASY**
MAKES: **4**
VEGETARIAN

ICE-CREAM COOKIE SANDWICH

Since when did sandwiches get capped at salad and bread? RELAX. This cookie ice-cream sando will have the SWEET ONES drooling. No ragrets. For the sweeeet ice-cream filling, our faves are cookie dough, vanilla or chocolate.

INGREDIENTS

½ cup (120 g) unsalted butter, at room temperature

¼ cup (50 g) light brown sugar

¼ cup (50 g) caster sugar

1 egg, plus 1 egg yolk, lightly beaten

1 teaspoon vanilla extract

1⅓ cups (160 g) all-purpose flour

½ teaspoon baking soda

generous pinch of salt

½ cup (90 g) chocolate chips

1 (1-pint [480-g]) paper tub ice cream

rainbow sprinkles, to serve

METHOD

1. Preheat the oven to 350°F (180°C, or gas mark 4). Line a baking sheet with parchment paper.
2. In a large bowl, combine the butter and both sugars until you have a smooth, thick paste. Add the eggs and vanilla and mix until smooth.
3. Sift in the flour, baking soda and salt, and mix once more. You should have a thick, sticky dough.
4. Fold in the chocolate chips and divide the cookie dough into 8 balls.
5. Lay the balls on the prepared baking sheet and bake for 12 minutes, or until the cookies have spread out and are cooked with a soft center.
6. Turn the tub of ice cream on its side and use a large, sharp knife to slice the ice cream into 4 rounds, tub and all, each about 1 to 2 inches (2.5 to 5 cm) thick. Peel away the carton from each slice and sandwich the ice-cream slices between the cookies.
7. Roll the edges of the cookie sandwiches in rainbow sprinkles and enjoy!

BANANA BOMB MUFFINS

PREP TIME: **10 MINUTES + FREEZING**

COOK TIME: **25 MINUTES**

DIFFICULTY: **EASY**

MAKES: **12**

VEGETARIAN

These muffins are DA BOMB. Take a bite and prepare for the oozing melted choco surprise.

INGREDIENTS

12 teaspoons chocolate hazelnut spread, such as Nutella

4 ripe bananas

⅓ cup (80 ml) vegetable oil

1 egg

⅓ cup (70 g) brown sugar

⅓ cup (80 ml) milk

1¾ cups (210 g) self-rising flour

1 teaspoon baking soda

METHOD

1. Spoon each teaspoon measure of the hazelnut spread separately on a plate, so each forms a "truffle." Place in the freezer to chill for half an hour until solid.
2. Preheat the oven to 375°F (190°C, or gas mark 5) and line a muffin pan with 12 muffin liners.
3. Peel 3 of the bananas and mash in a large mixing bowl, then add the oil, egg, sugar and milk and mix until you have a smooth, runny batter.
4. Sift in the flour and baking soda and fold until well combined.
5. Divide the mixture among the prepared muffin liners. Push a solid hazelnut-spread truffle into each, ensuring the truffles are fully submerged.
6. Top each muffin with a slice of the remaining banana and bake for 20–25 minutes until risen and golden with an oozing center. Enjoy while still warm.

CAUGHT'S CARROT CUPCAKES

PREP TIME: **10 MINUTES + CHILLING**
COOK TIME: **25 MINUTES**
DIFFICULTY: **EASY**
MAKES: **12**
VEGAN

The best way to eat carrots is in cupcake form. Fact.

INGREDIENTS

For the icing

1 cup (240 g) vegan non-dairy spread/margarine

3⅓ cups (400 g) powdered sugar

2 tablespoons plant-based milk

1 teaspoon vanilla extract

1 tablespoon freshly squeezed orange juice

For the cupcakes

2 large carrots, peeled

juice of ¼ lemon

½ cup (120 ml) vegetable oil

⅓ cup (80 ml) plant-based milk

1 cup (200 g) light brown sugar

1¾ cups (210 g) all-purpose flour

1 teaspoon baking powder

1 teaspoon ground cinnamon

⅓ cup (50 g) chopped walnuts, plus more to decorate (optional)

METHOD

1. To make the icing, put the vegan spread, powdered sugar, milk, vanilla extract and freshly squeezed orange juice into a large bowl and whisk for 1-2 minutes until light, fluffy and holding its shape. Cover and set aside in the refrigerator to chill.
2. Preheat the oven to 350°F (180°C, or gas mark 4) and line a muffin pan with 12 cupcake liners.
3. Finely grate one-fourth of a carrot. Squeeze the lemon juice over the top to stop the grated carrot from discoloring, then cover and set aside in the refrigerator. (This will be used to garnish the cupcakes.)
4. Grate the remaining carrot, using the coarse side of the grater for chunkier pieces. Put into a large mixing bowl and combine with the vegetable oil, plant milk and light brown sugar.
5. Sift in the all-purpose flour, baking powder and cinnamon and stir until well combined. Fold in the chopped walnuts, if using.
6. Spoon the cake batter into the prepared cupcake liners. Bake for 25 minutes until risen and golden.
7. Remove from the oven and transfer the cupcakes to a wire rack to cool. When cool, smooth a spoonful of icing over the top of each cupcake and garnish with the reserved carrot and chopped walnuts, if using. Serve immediately, or store in an airtight container in the refrigerator for up to 3 days.

PREP TIME: **15 MINUTES**
COOK TIME: **15 MINUTES**
DIFFICULTY: **EASY**
SERVES: **4**
VEGETARIAN

JAFFA CAKE BREAD & BUTTER PUDDING

Bread-and-butter pudding ELEVATED with a little jaffa cake goodness; you'll have the gang lining up down your road for a piece of this pud.

INGREDIENTS

2 tablespoons (30 g) salted butter, at room temperature

1 small brioche loaf, thickly sliced

20 jaffa cakes

2 cups (480 ml) custard

2 eggs, lightly beaten

⅓ cup (80 ml) milk

1 tablespoon powdered sugar, to dust (optional)

METHOD

1. Preheat the oven to 350°F (180°C, or gas mark 4).
2. Butter the slices of brioche and cut them in half diagonally. Stand the triangular slices upright in an 8-inch (20-cm) square baking pan and arrange the jaffa cakes in between. Reserve 2-3 jaffa cakes to crumble over the top.
3. In a medium bowl, combine 1⅔ cups (400 ml) of the custard with the eggs and milk, whisking to a smooth batter. Pour this over the brioche slices and jaffa cakes.
4. Chop up the reserved jaffa cakes and sprinkle over the top.
5. Cover with foil and bake for 10 minutes, then remove the foil and return to the oven for a further 2-5 minutes. The brioche should be lightly crisp and golden and the chocolate on the jaffa cakes melting.
6. Dust over the powdered sugar, if you like, and serve with the remaining custard poured over.

TIRAMISU BROWNIE BITES

PREP TIME: **30 MINUTES + COOLING + CHILLING**

COOK TIME: **25 MINUTES**

DIFFICULTY: **EASY**

MAKES: **16**

VEGETARIAN

As if brownies could be ANY MORE sensational... they can! Especially when a little juice is involved, you get me? Tiramisu means "pick me up" and trust, these bites will bring good vibes.

INGREDIENTS

For the brownies

5 tablespoons (75 g) salted butter, cubed

3½ ounces (100 g) dark chocolate, roughly chopped

½ cup (100 g) caster sugar

7 tablespoons (105 ml) coffee liqueur, suitable for vegetarians

1 egg, plus 1 egg yolk, lightly beaten

⅓ cup (40 g) all-purpose flour

For the rest

1¼ cups (300 ml) heavy cream

½ cup (120 g) mascarpone

2 tablespoons (25 g) powdered sugar

½ (7-ounce [210-g]) package ladyfingers (about 18)

⅔ cup (160 ml) strong espresso coffee, cooled to room temperature

cocoa powder, to dust

METHOD

1. Preheat the oven to 350°F (180°C, or gas mark 4). Line a an 8-inch (20-cm) square brownie pan with parchment paper.
2. Melt the butter and chocolate together in a heatproof bowl set over a saucepan of gently simmering water, making sure the bowl does not touch the water. Once melted, remove the bowl from the heat and stir in the caster sugar and half the coffee liqueur.
3. Allow the mixture to cool a little, then stir in the eggs and flour, ensuring the mixture is smooth.
4. Transfer the mixture to the prepared pan and bake for 20–25 minutes, or until a skewer inserted into the middle comes out clean. Allow the brownie to cool in the pan.
5. Put the cream, mascarpone, remaining liqueur and powdered sugar into a large bowl and whip for about 1 minute, or until thick and holding its shape.
6. Dip the ladyfingers in the espresso and lay across the top of the cooled brownies, still in the pan. Spoon over the boozy cream mixture and dust with cocoa powder.
7. Chill in the refrigerator, removing 30 minutes before serving. Slice into 16 small squares and enjoy!

PREP TIME: **10 MINUTES + FREEZING**

COOK TIME: **NONE**

DIFFICULTY: **EASY**

SERVES: **4**

VEGETARIAN

NO-CHURN ICE CREAM

Who has time to be churning ice cream? Once you make this, you'll want to quit the day job and get your own ice-cream van.

INGREDIENTS

½ cup (60 g) chocolate milkshake powder

¾ cup (180 ml) condensed milk

2½ cups (600 ml) heavy cream

To serve (optional)

chocolate sauce

salted caramel sauce

maraschino cherries

METHOD

1. Put the chocolate milkshake powder, condensed milk and heavy cream into a large mixing bowl and whip for about 5 minutes using an electric mixer, until thick. Transfer the mixture to a loaf pan and store in the freezer for 6 hours, or until frozen.
2. Serve in scoops, drizzled with chocolate and salted caramel sauce, and topped with maraschino cherries, if you like.

PREP TIME: **20 MINUTES + FREEZING**
COOK TIME: **10 MINUTES**
DIFFICULTY: **EASY**
MAKES: **10–12**
VEGAN

WATERMELON ICE POPS

Whip up some summer VIBES with these fruity frozen watermelon pops! Store in the freezer for them tropical days. You'll need ice pop molds and wooden popsicle sticks for these.

INGREDIENTS

⅓ cup (65 g) caster sugar
3 tablespoons (45 ml) water
1 baby watermelon (approx. 2¼ pounds [1 kg]
4 kiwis

METHOD

1. Put the sugar into a small saucepan. Add the water and give the pan a gentle shake to ensure that the sugar and water are spread evenly across the bottom. Place the saucepan over low heat and allow the sugar to melt. *Do not stir* or the sugar may crystallize, leaving you with a cloudy syrup. After 5–10 minutes, the sugar should have dissolved into the water, giving a clear liquid. Set aside.
2. Cut the watermelon in half and spoon out the flesh into a food processor. Pour in the sugar syrup and blend until smooth.
3. Pour the watermelon purée into ice-pop molds, leaving a gap of about ¾ inch (2 cm) at the top for the kiwi purée. Push in the popsicle sticks and put in the freezer to chill for 2 hours.
4. Meanwhile, rinse out the food processor, then cut the kiwis in half, spoon out the flesh into the food processor and blend to a smooth, thick purée. Set aside in the refrigerator until the ice pops have started to set.
5. Spoon the kiwi purée into the ice-pop molds over the watermelon and return to the freezer for a further 6 hours, or overnight. Serve and chill.

TIP:
Don't have ice-pop molds? Use small glasses instead.

RECLAIMED VINTAGE

CAUGHT SIPPIN'

CAUGHT DRINKIN' GAMES

Turn up (responsibly) at the shubz with Caught's favorite drinking games.

FIVES

Get the group sitting in a circle, each with one hand in a fist in the middle like spiritual tings.

Take it in turns to say a multiple of five (up to the number of people present, so if you have three players the max is 15, for four players the max is 20, and so on). The person guessing says their number on the count of three, at the same time that everyone either opens up their hands or keeps them clenched.

Open hands = 5, closed fists = 0.

If you guess the correct number, you're out of the game, but if you're incorrect, you must drink, and carry on playing.

If you're the last person in the game, you have to drink five fingers of your drink. It's a bit nuts, I can't lie.

TOP TIP: PRACTICE YOUR TIMES TABLES, YOU GET ME!

THE KILLER GAME

Bring your inner assassin to the shubz with this brutal (but 100 percent safe) murder game.

Fill three hats with the names of people who are playing, objects and locations in the house. Pick one of each. Now "kill" the person whose name you chose by handing them the object you picked in the location you chose without them realizing. Think Cluedo tings, but more interactive.

WARNING: THIS GAME MAY GO ON FOR THE LONGEST.

BACK TO BACK

Time to dig all the madness you wouldn't dare to share sober.

Get two of your mates standing back to back and ask them questions. Go easy with "Who is older?" or go in for a roast with "Who has the deadest dress sense?"

Whoever thinks they are the answer needs to drink, not speak; if neither of them, or both of them, drink, they both have to drink again.

TOP TIP: THIS IS FUN WITH BEST MATES, COUPLES, ALMOST-COUPLES, EX-COUPLES, OR ANYONE WITH SOME UNRESOLVED BEEF.

BITES 'N' BEER PONG

Beer Pong meets *Man v. Food*.

Put a fun twist on a firm favorite by adding bowls of food into your beer-cup formation on a table. Throw a ping-pong ball—from the other end of the table—aiming at the bowls and cups. Then drink (or eat) what you landed in.

Make it nasty (with inspo from our ILLEGAL food combos on Caught Snackin's YouTube) or keep it nice—up to you...

WARNING: THE WORSE THE FOOD COMBOS, THE MORE MATES YOU'LL LOSE.

THE HAT GAME

Fan of charades? Get ready for the level up.

Get into teams and fill a hat with names (think celebs, or spice it up by choosing people in the group). Take it in turns to pick out names and act out or describe the person (without saying their name). Get your team to guess as many as they can in a minute.

Not as much of a mazza as the killer game (*above left*), but definitely sure to stress a few man out.

WARNING: MAY CAUSE BEEF AT THE SHUBZ.

FLIP CUP

Yeah, people train for the Olympics... But no sport is as extreme as Flip Cup. THIS IS SERIOUS.

Split the group into two teams (keep those athletic ones on your side). Fill your cups in two rows along either side of the table and stand behind them.

The first member of each team must down their drink, and put their empty cup upside down over the edge of the table. They then need to use the back of their hand to flip the cup so it's the right way up on the table, before the next person can down their drink and repeat. The team to finish first wins.

WARNING: I BEG YOU GUYS, DON'T PLAY THIS WITH GLASS CUPS.

DON'T SAY IT

This one's easy, but effective.

Write up a list of words that are banned for the evening (use our glossary, on pages 8–9, if you want). Every time someone says one of those words, they have to drink.

TOP TIP: INCLUDE WORDS LIKE "DRINK," "GLASS," "FOOD," "MEAL" FOR MAXIMUM RESULTS, AND YOU'LL BE DRUNK BEFORE THE MAIN COURSE. (BUT PLZ BE CAREFUL.)

DISHWASHER GUMMY-BEAR VODKA

PREP TIME: **10 MINUTES + DISHWASHER CYCLE + CHILLING**

COOK TIME: **NONE**

DIFFICULTY: **EASY**

MAKES: **25 SHOTS**

VEGETARIAN

If you guys follow us on TikTok, you'll know about this MAD cheeky bev! However, the gummy bears be making a cameo appearance! Sweet and strong. Just like me.

INGREDIENTS

1 (700-ml) bottle vodka, suitable for vegetarians

14 ounces (400 g) vegetarian gummy bears, or your favorite gummy sweets

METHOD

1. Measure 1¼ cups (300 ml) of the vodka into a spare jar or bottle and keep for another occasion. This will allow space for the gummy bears.
2. Push the gummy bears into the vodka bottle and secure the lid.
3. Place the bottle in an empty dishwasher and run it on a "quick" or "eco" cycle, without using dishwasher detergent.
4. The dishwasher cycle will heat the vodka without cooking off the alcohol (important!) and allow the gummy bears to infuse and flavor the drink.
5. Chill before serving. There will be a bit of vodka-infused-melted-gummy-bear-sugar-goo at the bottom of the bottle, so strain that out, if you like. Or not.

LEMON JELL-O SHOTS

PREP TIME: **10 MINUTES + CHILLING**

COOK TIME: **NONE**

DIFFICULTY: **EASY**

SERVES: **16 (makes 32 wedges)**

VEGETARIAN

Dangerously GOOD lemon Jell-O shots, slurped from lemon-skin cups to turn the level up at the shubz. Jell-O isn't usually suitable for vegetarians, so you'll have to look for vegetarian-friendly gelatin if you need these shots to be.

INGREDIENTS

8 lemons

1 (5-ounce [140-g]) package vegetarian lemon-flavored Jell-O

9½ ounces (285 ml) boiling water

4 ounces (120 ml) limoncello, suitable for vegetarians

METHOD

1. Cut the lemons in half lengthwise and carefully scoop out the flesh so that you are left with the hollow skins. Juice the flesh and save the juice for another occasion.
2. Place the Jell-O into a medium-sized bowl. Pour over the boiling water and stir until the Jell-O has dissolved. This should take about 5 minutes.
3. Stir in the limoncello and pour the mixture into the lemon-skin cups. Place in the refrigerator for at least 2½ hours to set.
4. Once set, slice each lemon cup in half to make lemon wedges.

TIP:
Throw some oranges and limes into the mix. Simply swap the Jell-O flavors accordingly or mix and match.

PREP TIME: **5 MINUTES EACH**

COOK TIME: **NONE**

DIFFICULTY: **EASY**

SERVES: **1**

VEGETARIAN

SPICY-HOT BLOODY MARY

Word on the street is that if you say "Bloody Mary" three times, a cocktail will appear! If it doesn't, then you shouldn't be so gullible; go make this recipe yourself.

INGREDIENTS

1 (1-ounce [30-g]) package spicy-hot corn puffs

juice of 1 lime

handful of ice

1½ ounces (45 ml) vodka, suitable for vegetarians

½ teaspoon hot sauce

½ teaspoon vegetarian Worcestershire sauce

¼ teaspoon pepper

6 ounces (180 ml) tomato juice

1 celery stalk

METHOD

1. Set aside a small handful of spicy-hot corn puffs to garnish and crush the rest into crumbs with a rolling pin. Put the spicy crumbs in a dish.
2. Squeeze half the lime juice onto a small plate and dip the rim of a tall glass in the juice, then dip it into the spicy-hot crumbs.
3. Fill the glass with ice and add the vodka, hot sauce, Worcestershire sauce, pepper and tomato juice. Give it a stir with a stick of celery and enjoy!

Cocktails, cocktails, cocktails

RUM & COKE FLOAT

Get merry with this cheeky float. The sugary kick with the booze will make for some swashbuckling scenes, trust...

INGREDIENTS

large handful of crushed ice

1½ ounces (45 ml) dark rum, suitable for vegetarians

10 ounces (300 ml) cola

2 scoops vanilla ice cream

maraschino cherry and lemon slice, to garnish (optional)

METHOD

1. Put the crushed ice into a tall glass and pour in the dark rum.
2. Top up with the cola and vanilla ice cream.
3. Garnish with a cherry and a slice of lemon, if you like.

ENERGY MOJITO

Those days where you're flagging at 5 p.m. ... This energy mojito will bring you right back to life, feeling the buzz.

INGREDIENTS

juice of 2 limes, plus a lime slice, to serve

½ teaspoon sugar

3 mint sprigs

handful of crushed ice

1½ ounces (45 ml) white rum, suitable for vegetarians

8 ounces (240 ml) energy drink

METHOD

1. Put the lime juice, sugar and mint leaves from 2 of the mint sprigs into a small bowl and crush with the end of a rolling pin until you have a loose, paste-like consistency.
2. Scoop a handful of crushed ice into a tall glass and pour over the mint mixture, followed by the white rum and the energy drink.
3. Give the mojito a good stir and garnish with the remaining mint sprig and the lime slice.

RUM & COKE
FLOAT

CINEMA SLUSHY

PREP TIME: **15 MINUTES + CHILLING**

COOK TIME: **NONE**

DIFFICULTY: **EASY**

SERVES: **2**

VEGETARIAN

A RAINBOW slushy to complete your movie night at home. Vibrant, fruity and the perfect complement to your popcorn, G—get on it!

INGREDIENTS

1½ cups (360 g) ice cubes
4 (3-ounce [84-g]) lemon-flavored ice pops
5 ounces (150 ml) red, cherry-flavored soda
1 teaspoon pink food coloring
5 ounces (150 ml) blue-colored soda
1 teaspoon blue food coloring
2 cherries, to garnish

METHOD

1. Wrap the ice cubes in a clean tea towel and bash with a rolling pin to crush into small pieces.
2. For the cherry-flavored slushy, put 2 of the ice pops (sticks removed) into a food processor with half the crushed ice, the cherry soda and the pink food coloring. Purée the mixture repeatedly, in 5-second blasts, until you have a thick, slushy consistency. Transfer the mixture to a container and place in the freezer to chill while you make the blue slushy.
3. Repeat the process with the remaining ice pops and ice, blue-colored soda and blue food coloring.
4. Serve the slushies, layered up, in 2 tall glasses. Finish with a cherry and serve immediately.

MINT-CHOC FREAKSHAKE

PREP TIME: **15 MINUTES + CHILLING**

COOK TIME: **5 MINUTES**

DIFFICULTY: **EASY**

SERVES: **2**

VEGETARIAN

This shake gets pretty freaky. Mint on mint action with this SWEET ONE. Mint chocolate balls, mint ice cream, mint chocolate cookies… Did we mention there's mint in here?

INGREDIENTS

- 3½ ounces (100 g) dark chocolate, roughly chopped
- 2 (3-ounce [90-g]) packages peppermint-flavored chocolate bubbles, such as Aero Bubbles
- 4 tablespoons rainbow sprinkles
- 5 scoops mint chocolate chip ice cream
- 7 ounces (210 ml) milk
- whipped cream
- 2–4 mint chocolate-coated cookie candy bars, such as Kit Kats

METHOD

1. Melt the chocolate in a heatproof bowl set over a saucepan of gently simmering water, making sure the bowl does not touch the water. This should take about 5 minutes.
2. Crush 1 package of peppermint-flavored chocolate bubbles with a rolling pin, then place the pieces in a dish with the rainbow sprinkles.
3. Dip the rims of 2 tall glasses into the melted chocolate, then roll the rims in the dish to coat the chocolate with the bubbles and sprinkles. Carefully drizzle the remaining melted chocolate around the insides of the glasses. Place the glasses in the refrigerator to chill.
4. Put the remaining package of mint-chocolate bubbles in a high-powered blender. Top with 3 scoops of the ice cream and the milk. Blend until smooth, then pour into the prepared glasses.
5. Top each glass with another scoop of ice cream, whipped cream, more crushed mint-chocolate bubbles and mint-chocolate candies, halved lengthways if you like. Serve immediately!

FROZEN

PASSION FRUIT MARTINI

These will BLESS your summer vacay by the pool. And if you're not on vacation, then this drink is the closest you'll get.

INGREDIENTS

2 tropical fruit-flavor ice pops, such as Solero

½ mango, peeled and cubed

1½ ounces (45 ml) vodka, suitable for vegetarians

3½ ounces (100 ml) pineapple juice

1 passion fruit, halved

METHOD

1. Remove the sticks from the ice pops and put them into a high-powered blender, along with the mango, vodka and pineapple juice. Blend until smooth, then strain into 2 glasses.
2. Top each with a passion fruit half and enjoy.

FROZEN

ESPRESSO MARTINI

Ice-cold voddy coffee sprinkled with cocoa? Yes plz.

INGREDIENTS

3½ ounces (100 ml) strong espresso coffee

large handful of crushed ice

1½ ounces (45 ml) vodka, suitable for vegetarians

3½ ounces (100 ml) coffee liqueur, suitable for vegetarians

2 tablespoons sugar

cocoa powder, to dust (optional)

METHOD

1. Brew the espresso coffee and allow it to cool to room temperature.
2. Put the crushed ice, vodka, coffee liqueur, sugar and cooled coffee into a food processor or high-powered blender. Purée in 5-second blasts until well combined.
3. Divide between 2 glasses and dust with cocoa powder, if you like.

Best sipped in the sunshine, but these taste great whatever the weather

PREP TIME: **5 MINUTES EACH**
COOK TIME: **NONE**
DIFFICULTY: **EASY**
SERVES: **2**
VEGETARIAN

FROZEN PIÑA COLADA

If you like piña coladas... MAKE THIS. Pineapple and coconut rum blended with ice cream, topped with fruity garnish and of course a li'l umbrella for that beachside finesse.

INGREDIENTS

handful of crushed ice
1 cup (150 g) frozen pineapple chunks
5 ounces (150 ml) coconut rum liqueur, suitable for vegetarians
⅓ cup (80 g) vanilla ice cream

To garnish (optional)

2 pineapple wedges
2 maraschino cherries
pineapple leaves from a fresh pineapple
cocktail umbrellas

METHOD

1. Put the crushed ice, frozen pineapple, coconut rum liqueur and ice cream into a high-powered blender. Purée in 5-second blasts until well combined with a smooth, thick consistency.
2. Divide between 2 large glasses and garnish each with a pineapple wedge, a cherry, pineapple leaves and a snazzy umbrella, if you like.

FROZEN
PASSION FRUIT
MARTINI
FROZEN
ESPRESSO
MARTINI

FROZEN PIÑA COLADA

PREP TIME: **5 MINUTES**
COOK TIME: **2 MINUTES**
DIFFICULTY: **EASY**
SERVES: **2**
VEGETARIAN

HOT CHOCOLATE ORANGE MOCHA

When chocolate met orange, we were interested. When chocolate orange met coffee? Hold me back.

INGREDIENTS

10 ounces (300 ml) whole milk
1 chocolate orange, such as Terry's
2 shots espresso coffee
whipped cream

METHOD

1. Heat the milk in a small saucepan over low heat for 2 minutes.
2. Break up the chocolate orange and finely chop 1 of the segments, setting this aside for garnish.
3. Remove the saucepan from the heat and add the rest of the chocolate orange segments. Stir the chocolate into the hot milk until completely melted and combined.
4. Pour the espresso coffee into 2 glasses and top with the hot chocolate orange mixture.
5. Finish with whipped cream and the finely chopped chocolate.

STRAWBERRY RICE PAPER BUBBLE TEA

PREP TIME: **5 MINUTES**
COOK TIME: **15 MINUTES**
DIFFICULTY: **EASY**
SERVES: **2**
VEGETARIAN

Bubble tea is WAY easier than you think with this secret magic. Just be sure to have a wide straw to slurp them LOVELY BUBBLES.

INGREDIENTS

14 ounces (400 g) strawberries, stems removed, halved

2 tablespoons sugar

2 tablespoons water

4 sheets rice paper (sold as spring roll wrappers)

2 handfuls crushed ice

18 ounces (500 ml) milk

METHOD

1. Put the strawberries into a small saucepan with the sugar and water. Place over low heat and bring to a gentle simmer. Simmer for 10 minutes, until the strawberries have broken down to a soft, mushy consistency. Remove from the heat and allow to cool.
2. Meanwhile, dip each of the rice paper sheets in lukewarm water so that they become pliable. Roll each sheet up tightly and slice into small "boba" pieces, about ½ inch (1 cm) wide.
3. When the strawberry mixture has cooled, purée in a food processor or high-powered blender until smooth. Pass the strawberry mixture through a sieve to remove any seeds.
4. Return the strained strawberry mixture to the small saucepan and add the rice paper boba. Simmer for 5 minutes. The boba will take on the pink color of the strawberry mixture.
5. Divide the boba mixture between 2 tall glasses and top with crushed ice. Finish with milk and a wide straw to drink the bubble tea. Serve immediately!

TIP:
Biodegradable or reusable bubble tea straws are widely available online.

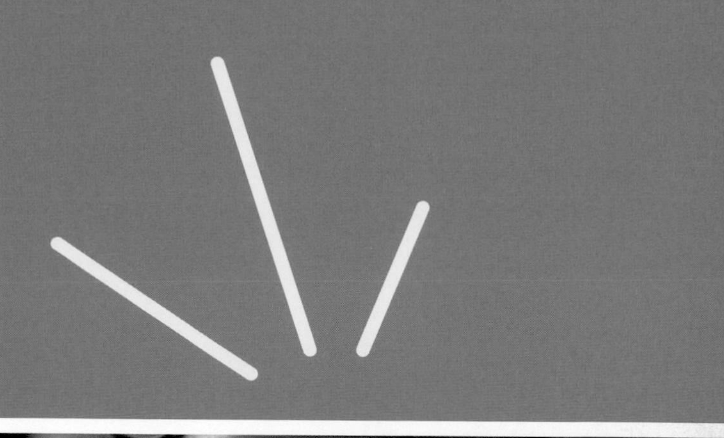

INDEX

ACKNOWLEDGMENTS

BIG LOVE to our agents Lauren and Jo for believing in the Caught cookbook dream! When we first started playing around with recipes on TikTok, we never imagined they'd end up in a REAL-LIFE cookbook. MADNESS! Shoutout Lauren and Jo for making it happen for real!

But we couldn't have got here without the gang behind the scenes. Many blessings to Jason, Freya, Lydia, Harleigh and the whole Caught Snackin' team, who've worked so hard cooking and creating to bring this book to life.